LIFE OF CONGREVE.

LIFE

OF

WILLIAM CONGREVE

BY

EDMUND GOSSE, M.A.

KENNIKAT PRESS
Port Washington, N. Y./London

LIFE OF WILLIAM CONGREVE

First published in 1888
Reissued in 1972 by Kennikat Press
Library of Congress Catalog Card No: 77-153215
ISBN 0-8046-1525-X

Manufactured by Taylor Publishing Company Dallas, Texas

CONTENTS.

—⬥⬥—

CHAPTER I.

CHAPTER II.

PREFATORY NOTE.

THIS is the first time that any attempt has been made to write a detailed biography of Congreve, and that circumstance may be held to excuse the intrusion of what is commonly dispensed with in the volumes of this series—a lengthy prefatory note. There can be no question that, unless fresh material should most unexpectedly turn up, the opportunity for preparing a full and picturesque life of this poet has wholly passed away. The task should have been undertaken a hundred and fifty years ago, when those were still alive who had known him personally. This occasion was unaccountably allowed to slip by, partly, no doubt, because the modern art of biography was but very poorly understood, but partly, also, because Congreve was no very fascinating or absorbing human being. Correct biographies of Pope or Swift were not published until long after the decease of those writers, yet we have no difficulty whatever in restoring them to life in fancy. But then they possessed an interesting personal quality, of which the author of *The Way of the World* seems to have been devoid.

In 1730, the year after Congreve's death, that audacious

pirate Curll issued a volume entitled *Memoirs of the Life, Writings, and Amours of William Congreve, Esq.* He had the effrontery to invite Mrs. Bracegirdle to contribute facts to it; in refusing, that admirable actress predicted that the book would not have "a new sheet" in it. She might safely have said "a new page." It is an absolutely worthless construction of scissors and paste, containing nothing previously unprinted, except one or two lies, and it is mainly occupied either with reprints of Congreve's scattered minor writings or with gossip absolutely foreign to his career. The name of Charles Wilson appears on the title of this wretched forgery; it is understood that there never existed such a person, and it has been conjectured that it was John Oldmixon, "that virulent party writer for hire," who was the guilty hack.

The publication of these spurious *Memoirs* seems to have dissuaded any honest writer from undertaking in earnest the task which "Charles Wilson" pretended to have carried out. At all events, no life of Congreve has appeared since that date, until the present volume. The best account of Congreve, published during the age after his death, is the article by Dr. Campbell in the *Biographica Britannica.* Campbell can scarcely have known Congreve personally, but he was helped by the aged Southerne, who had been Congreve's friend from college onwards, and who supplied him with notes. In later times the known particulars of his life have been more or less accurately summarized and added to by Dr. Samuel Johnson, Leigh Hunt, and Macaulay. The portion of an essay which the last-mentioned writer dedicates to Congreve is well known, and is so admirable that we regret that Macaulay never returned to treat Vanbrugh and Farquhar in the same broad and sympathetic spirit. Thackeray's more brilliant essay is much less accurate than Macaulay's. It must be read for the pleasure such beautiful imaginative writing gives, but not as a portrait of the veritable Congreve.

None of these accounts of Congreve, however, extends beyond the limits of a very few pages, and, extraordinary as it seems, in these days of research, no one till now has taken the trouble to examine the existing sources of information, and collect the facts still discoverable about the greatest of our comic dramatists. I have not attempted to make a hero of this unromantic, "unreproachful" bard; I shall be satisfied if I have succeeded in surveying rather minutely a little province of our literary history which had been neglected, and in so adding my small contribution to the materials of criticism. Some fallacies I think I have destroyed; the theory of Congreve's magnificent and preposterous wealth in early life is shown to be without a basis, and I hope it will be acknowledged that as we know him more intimately he turns out to be more amiable and much less cynical than he had been depicted to us. But I am very far from pretending that he was one of those whom, in the phrase so persistently and falsely attributed to him, "to love is a liberal education."

The story of this book is compiled from materials scattered over a great many volumes, not all of which are to be found in any single library. Among the more obvious sources of information I may mention Cibber, Giles Jacob, Malone's Dryden, Spence's *Anecdotes*, Swift's correspondence, George-Monck Berkeley's curious and valuable volume, Luttrel's *Diary*, and the newspapers of the day. I am glad to be able, for the first time, to chronicle the exact date of the publication of almost all Congreve's writings. The bibliography of this poet, crowded as it mainly is into a short span of years, had hitherto been entirely neglected ; this is a small matter, perhaps, but not to be despised in dealing with such masterpieces as the great comedies of Congreve. I may be allowed to call attention to the chapter on the Collier controversy. This is the first time in which the pamphlets which were provoked by that interesting crisis in our literary ethics have been successively examined and chronologically arranged.

From the minor and less attainable writings of Congreve I have occasionally quoted. But I have thought it needless to pad out the limited space at my disposal by citing passages from the great comedies, more especially as the text of these is now at the command of every reader. Only last year there appeared an excellent text of Congreve's Plays, in the Mermaid Series (Vizetelly & Co.), at a low price. To this edition the Congreve section of Macaulay's Essay was prefixed, and Mr. A. C. Ewald appended a few valuable notes.

LIFE OF CONGREVE.

CHAPTER I.

OF all the important men of letters born after the Restoration, the earliest to distinguish himself was William Congreve, and with him, in a certain sense, the literature of the eighteenth century began. He was the most eminent poet between Dryden and Pope, and he formed the advanced guard of the army of the Age of Anne. Like other writers of his time—like Gay, for instance, and Steele—he lost count of his years, and thought, or affected to think, that he was younger than we know him to have been. In contradiction to the general impression of his friends, however, he maintained that the event took place in England, not in Ireland; he was right, but this fact was not proved until the close of last century. Theophilus Cibber, and others following him, have asserted that Sir James Ware reckoned Congreve among writers born in Ireland, on evidence received from Southerne. There is some mystification here, for Sir James Ware died before our poet was born, and the enlarged edition of his book, published long afterwards by Walter Harris, gives no authority of Southerne's for including Congreve among Irish worthies. It seems indubitable that Congreve thought that he was not born until 1672, and early biographers, with more evidence before them than we possess, may have discovered that, by that time, the Congreve family had migrated to Youghal.

The family of the poet was ancient and of high repute. It took its name from Congreve, a hamlet one mile south-west of the town of Pentridge, in the west of Staffordshire. At Stretton Hall, a mile or two further in the country, in the midst of land which is still agricultural, the Congreves had resided since the beginning of the fourteenth century. Richard Congreve, the poet's grandfather, had been one of the thirteen veteran cavaliers destined by Charles II. for the order of the Royal Oak, if that design had ever been completed. His second son, William Congreve, is said to have married Anne, daughter of Sir Thomas, and granddaughter of the famous Sir Anthony Fitzherbert. But in 1670 Sir Anthony had been dead more than one hundred and thirty years, so that there is obviously here some mistake, and other authorities say that the poet's mother bore the maiden name of Browning. The Fitzherberts were a very extensive Staffordshire family, and both stories may be partly true; or Anne may have been the wife of Richard, not of William. The poet was born at Bardsey, near Leeds, in the house of his maternal great-uncle, Sir John Lewis. His baptism was entered in the parish register of Bardsey, where it was discovered by Malone, under the date February 10, 1669 [1670].

William Congreve the elder was an officer in the army,

and during the infancy of the poet he removed, with his family, to command the garrison of the town of Youghal, in Ireland. According to Southerne, he resigned this office after three years, to become agent for the estates of the Earl of Cork, and thenceforward resided at Lismore, as the centre of the Burlington interests. But in 1685 we find him still described as "de Yogholia." It was probably in the year 1681 that the younger William Congreve proceeded to the Eton of Ireland, Kilkenny, where one of his schoolfellows was Jonathan Swift, three years his senior. It may be questioned whether the friendship that existed throughout the life of Congreve between these two great men began at school or at college, since Swift left Kilkenny as early as April 24, 1682. It is, however, distinctly stated that Congreve "received the first tincture of letters at the great school of Kilkenny." He was noted as a boy of talent. "While at school he gave several instances of his genius for poetry; but the most peculiar one was a very pretty copy of verses which he made upon the Death of his Master's Magpie." These have not survived, and the earliest verses of his which we possess are the "Ah! whither, whither shall I fly!" attributed to 1687. His tutor at Kilkenny was Dr. Hinton.

On the 5th of April, 1685, Congreve proceeded to Trinity College, Dublin, where his tutor was St. George Ashe, the eminent mathematician. This distinguished man, then quite young, and but recently elected to a fellowship, is remembered less from the fact that he afterwards adorned three successive Irish dioceses, than from his intimacy with Swift, whom he is said, long afterwards, to have secretly married to Stella. Congreve's college record was probably a better one than Swift's, for he not only became a fine scholar, but, according to Southerne, enjoyed that reputation at Trinity. He was certainly not less attracted by the rumours of poetical, and especially dramatic, fame left behind them or sent backward in reverberation by various graduates slightly senior to himself, especially Nahum Tate and Thomas Southerne. At all events, in spite of the "somebody tells us" of Leigh Hunt, Congreve and Swift were certainly together, as the register of the college testifies, under the literature-loving Dr. Ashe. If the early report that *Incognita* was written in a fortnight, at the age of seventeen, be correct, this novel was a product of the poet's last year at college. At the close of 1688, like Swift, and possibly in his company, Congreve hastened into England at the desire of his father, Ireland being now, after the Revolution, no place where a gentleman whose family had served the Stuarts could feel comfortable or hope for promotion.

Before accompanying Congreve across the channel we may briefly chronicle the fate of his first work. The original edition of *Incognita: or, Love and Duty Reconciled* appears to be extremely rare. As a matter of fact I have been able to trace but one copy of it, that in the Bodleian.[1] It was licensed December 22, 1691, and published, according to an advertisement in the *London Gazette*, on the 25th of February, 1692. *Incognita* seems to have enjoyed considerable popularity. It was in-

[1] Incognita : or, Love and Duty Reconciled. A Novel. Printed for Peter Buck, at the Sign of the Temple, near Temple Bar in Fleet Street, 1692.

cluded by the publisher, R. Wellington, in a series of cheap reprints of novels, which he issued in 1700. This had neither Congreve's name upon it, nor the pseudonym Cleophil which signed the original issue, and it was equally without preface or dedication. In the Dyce and Forster Libraries two separate editions of 1713 contain all of these. There were probably several other issues of *Incognita*, besides the reprint of 1730. That an edition of an anonymous novel of the end of the seventeenth century should have disappeared is no matter for surprise. This class of literature was treated with marked disdain, and having been read to pieces by the women, was thrown into the fire. If the novels of the great Mrs. Behn had not been collected, many of them would now scarcely be known to exist, and the British Museum has not, hitherto, been able to secure any edition of them all earlier than the fifth.

In a courtly dedication to Mrs. Katherine Leveson, the author of *Incognita* shows himself already an adept in that elegant and elaborate persiflage which later on became a second nature to him :—

> Since I have drawn my pen (he says) at a *Recontro*, I think it better to engage, where, though there be still enough to disarm me, there is too much generosity to wound; for so shall I have the saving reputation of an unsuccessful courage, if I can't make it a drawn battle. But methinks the comparison intimates something of a defiance, and savours of arrogance, wherefore, since I am conscious to myself of a fear which I can't put off, let me use the policy of cowards, and lay this novel, unarm'd, naked and shivering, at your feet, so that if it should want merit to challenge protection, yet, as an object of charity, it may move compassion.

It is impossible for the present writer to agree with the

critics who have passed over this novel in contemptuous silence or with a word of dispraise. It is a slight and immature production, no doubt, but it is far from being without merit, and in relation to Congreve's subsequent dramatic work it deserves a close examination. In 1691 Mrs. Aphra Behn had passed away, and no praise is due to Cleophil for having followed her in substituting the short novel of intrigue for the long-winded and interminable romance of the Scudéry and Calprenède School. But it is noticeable that while the latter was still in full favour with the public, Congreve saw the ridiculous side of a fashion which could not prepare its readers in less than ten enormous volumes for the nuptials of the illustrious Aronce and the admirable Clélie. He says:—

> Romances are generally composed of the constant loves and invincible courages of heroes, heroines, kings and queens, mortals of the first rank, and so forth; where lofty language, miraculous contingencies, and impossible performances, elevate and surprise the reader into a giddy delight, which leaves him flat upon the ground wherever he leaves off, and vexes him to think how he has suffered himself to be pleased and transported, concerned and afflicted at . . . knights' success, and damsels' misfortunes, and such like, when he is forced to be very well convinced that 'tis all a lie.

He argues against the adoption of so bewildering a style of fiction, and is all in favour of such realism in novel-writing as "not being wholly unusual or unprecedented may, by not being so distant from our belief, bring also the pleasure nearer to us." This, the best stories of Mrs. Behn, with all their obvious faults, did strive to do, pointing with a trembling hand towards the downright forgeries of real life to be introduced in the next generation by Defoe. The interest of *Incognita*, however, lies for us, not in its artificial and but faintly entertaining story, but in the instinctive art by which the author, a dramatist to the finger-tips, has seized and elaborated those parts of the story only which bear a theatrical interpretation, and has made his book less a novel than a scenario. He introduces his personages only when they can be confronted as if upon the stage, and is mainly concerned to preserve "the unity of contrivance."

As *Incognita* has long ceased to be easily accessible, some outline of its contents may here be permitted. According to a writer in the *Biographia Britannica*, the events described, although the action is laid in Italy, took place in England; this seems very improbable, however, and if Congreve had taken the trouble to write a *roman à clef*, some gossip, we may be sure, would have preserved the key. Any one who chooses may, if he likes, see Swift in the Hippolito and Congreve himself in the Aurelian of this probable tale. Aurelian and Hippolito, a young gentleman for whom he had contracted an intimate friendship, are educated together in Sienna; at the command of Aurelian's father, both proceed to Florence to improve their studies, Florence being the home of the old man in question. On arriving the youths discover that a court ball is arranged for the same evening, and accordingly they determine not to report themselves, but to attend that night at the palace in disguise. By the help of their servants they procure splendid costumes for the evening, but Hippolito has to put up with the dress of a certain cavalier of fashion who happens to be ill in bed. At the ball, of course, each of the young men falls violently in love with a mask, and the sallies and rallies of their courteous impertinence read exactly like what we should expect in the first lispings of a comic dramatist. Here is a specimen :—

This raillery awakened the cavalier from the agreeable reverie he was fallen into.

"'Tis true, madam !" cried he, "but as you justly observed, the invention may be foreign to the person who puts it in practice ; and, as well as I love a good dress, I should be loath to answer for the wit of all around us."

"I hope then," returned the lady, "you are convinced of your error, since 'tis impossible to say who in all this assembly made choice of their own fancy or their friends ?"

"Not in the least," said he, "I dare engage that lady who is playing with the tassels of her girdle, though she is agreeably dressed, does not know it."

"You are not mistaken in your guess," cried she, smiling, "for I assure you that lady knows as little as any in the room—except myself."

"Ah ! madam," said Aurelian, "you know everything save your own perfections, and those only you will not know, as 'tis the height of human wisdom to seem ignorant of them."

"How ?" cried the lady, "I thought the knowledge of one's self had most justly deserved that character ?"

Aurelian was a little at a loss how to recover the blunder, when the music coming in, luckily for him put a stop to the discourse.

Hippolito enjoys a more instant, but a more embarrassing conquest than Aurelian, for the lady he addresses, imagining him to be the gentleman whose costume he is wearing, warns him of his extreme rashness in appearing in that assembly, and urges him to follow her to a place of safety, which he does, but leaves her undiscovered, having secured her handkerchief. Aurelian, in his turn, not venturing to mention his own name, which was well known in Florence, calls himself Hippolito to the mask with whom he dances, while the real Hippolito can think of no better pseudonym for himself than Aurelian. Next day, in suits of silver armour enamelled with azure, the two young strangers, with their vizors down, tilt in the lists before the Duke, and, of course, win the honours of the field from the most gallant Florentines. Aurelian's lady, who calls herself Incognita, and who is really the fair Juliana, a lady of fortune whom Aurelian's father designs for his son's bride, follows them disguised to their lodgings; they are absent, but she finds a variety of other persons whom she is not seeking, as on the ordinary comic stage of the Restoration. Aurelian has an awful scene, meanwhile, in a churchyard, by night, with an assassin, and Hippolito gets into an apparently hopeless tangle of intrigue through being, by his own fault, mistaken for Aurelian. After a great many scenes, in which the prose dialogue totters on the very brink of such blank verse as Crowne and Settle boasted, the web is loosened and all the threads are drawn out. Each of the young men approaches the old gentleman on his knee, and receives the hand of the lady whom he desires, who turns out also to be his predestined bride, and so love and duty are reconciled. It would not make at all a bad little play, and some of the scenes are prettily described. More than this even a biographer dares not say in praise of Cleophil's *Incognita.*

There is reason to suppose that for the first two years after his leaving college, Congreve remained in Staffordshire with his relations. Probably the whole family returned to England, since the elder William Congreve, who had been described as "de Yogholia," in 1685, and of Lismore a little later, is once more "de Stratton in com. Staffordiæ," in 1691. Legend says that *The Old Bachelor* was written, some years before it was acted, in a garden. We shall not be far wrong if we conjecture that the date of its composition was the summer or early autumn of 1690. Congreve, who very rarely speaks of himself, gives us a precious fragment of autobiography while defending *The Old Bachelor* in the *Amendments* of 1698. He says, referring to Collier's attacks :—

> I cannot hold laughing when I compare his dreadful comment with such poor silly words as are in the text, especially when I reflect how young a beginner and how very much a boy I was when that Comedy was written, which several know was some years before it was acted. When I wrote it I had little thoughts of the stage, but did it to amuse myself in a slow recovery from a fit of sickness. Afterwards, through my indiscretion it was seen, and in some little time more it was acted.

Two beautiful manorial gardens dispute the honour of being the birth-place of *The Old Bachelor*, that of Stratton Hall, and that of Aldermaston, in Berkshire. It may be that the indisposition the poet describes was serious and lingering ; at all events, it was not until the subsequent winter had past that he made his start in life, arriving in London at the age of twenty-one. The Register of the Middle Temple notes the occurrence as follows :—

> Marte 17mo. 1690 [91]. Mr. Wilmūs. Congreve, filius et heres apparens Wilm̄i. Congreve de Stratton in com. Staffordiæ, Ar. admissus est in societatem Medii Templi, specialiter.

Congreve was not fitted for the plodding life of a professional man. His father, it is evident, had now inherited the family estates, and the young man's allowance was probably ample. "But the severe study of the law had so little relation to the active disposition and sprightly humour of the young gentleman, that though he continued for three or four years," that is to say, no doubt, until his civil-service appointment in July, 1695, "to live in chambers, and pass for a Templar, yet it does not appear that he ever applied himself with diligence to conquer his dislike to a course of life, which had been chosen for him with so little respect either to the turn of his natural parts or the preceding course of his education." The same contemporary evidence, however, asserts that he eagerly and industriously gave himself to a preparation for the literary life.

Between March, 1691, when he arrives, probably alone, in London, and August, 1692, when he is already an accepted poet and the friend of Dryden, there is a period of nearly a year and a half during which we see nothing of Congreve. He quickly took his place, we know, with that elegant adroitness which was his characteristic, in the frivolous London of William and Mary, that nucleus of the "Town" which revolved about the Court, which haunted the Park and the Play-house, and which lived mainly in the Coffee-houses. The Revolution had brought with it much less change of manners than might have been expected. Under the sullen patronage of James II., it is true, the fashions and politer arts had somewhat languished. But in 1690, when the turmoil of the change of dynasty had ceased, there came a reaction to the temper of Charles II. The Sir Foplings and Sir Courtlys, who had disappeared in the east wind of the ascetic days of James, began to sun themselves in the Mall again, the same delicious creatures, with their long fair wigs, and the *creve-cœur* locks curling on the napes of their soft necks, with their scarlet heels, and clouded canes, and laced handkerchiefs breathing the Montpellier essence or perfume of millefleur water, their gold boxes of *pastillios* in their hands, their elderly faces painted young with Spanish red and white ceruse, and the frangipan exhaling from the chicken-skin gloves upon their plump white hands. These were the Beaux, the pink of French affectation, the great heroic figures of the comedy of their age.

These were the heroes for whom life provided no loftier duty or more harassing care than the fit conduct of a spruce cravat-string or the judicious careening of a periwig. Noble creatures they were, scarcely willing to submit, in hurrying to an appointment, to allow their clothes to be pressed into "the scandal of a small sedan." They were the first objects of a playwright's study, and an Etheredge or a Crowne might rarely get any further. But Congreve was to fill his various stage with a multitude of other figures, personages made, no doubt, to circle around the central group of tyrant-beaux, but, in their own way, to be no less living and vivid. For this wider study of the comic side of life the Coffee-houses offered an extraordinary wealth of opportunity. Here men of all sorts met in the forenoon, and again, after the play, in the early evening, to talk, to discuss politics, to hear the last new thing. Here auctions were held;

hither came those who had lost such a valuable possession as "a small black groom, pock-marked, last seen in dark-red small-clothes;" those who were carrying on a clandestine correspondence which might not be pursued in their own house or lodgings. This hurly-burly, where courtiers, quacks, soldiers, knights, poets, and mountebanks, formed "a hotch-potch of society," was the representative of the modern club, without its restrictions and with five times its vivacity. The age, especially in London, was less domestic, had less of the snug ease of "home" and its familiar pleasures, than any before or since in England. The foreign habit of living in the *café* and the *restaurant* had been adopted in deliberate rejection of the Puritan home with its fireside-hearth, and this exotic fashion had not yet begun to lose its popularity.

A rare poem, *The School of Politicks*, published in 1690, gives a curious account of the humours of the Coffee-house as Congreve must have found them when he arrived in town. The company met to drink claret or a dish of tea:—

> The murmuring buzz which through the room was sent
> Did bee-hives' noise exactly represent,
> And like a bee-hive, too, 'twas filled, and thick,
> All tasting of the Honey Politick
> Called "news," which they all greedily sucked in.

The Coffee-house presented the ideal of good company, and without a modern snobishness, for, as has already been said, all classes of men who could pay, and who would behave decently, were admitted. The anonymous Pindaric bard just quoted proceeds:—

More various scenes of humour I might tell
Which in my little stay befell;
Such as grave wits, who, spending farthings four,
Sit, smoke, and warm themselves an hour;
Or modish town-sparks, drinking chocolate,
With beaver cocked, and laughing loud,
To be thought wits among the crowd,
Or sipping tea, while they relate
Their evening's frolic at the Rose.

This was the field, we cannot doubt, in which Congreve learned his art, whence he could conjure up the variegated mob that crowds his stage, where he listened to a whisper of that wit and intellectual passion which thrill his polished and artificial characters.

Congreve made his start in literary life — for the *Incognita* was scarcely a *début* — under the majestic auspices of Dryden. The young poet has a prominent place, and is introduced without apology, in the *Juvenal and Persius* of 1693. This book, a handsome folio, was ready for the press on the 18th of August, 1692, and, according to the *London Gazette*, in spite of the date on its title-page, was published on the 27th of October in that year. No better opportunity for making a public appearance could be conceived. This was, perhaps, the most important publication of 1692, and it was one in which Congreve found himself associated with the first poet of the age, and with a group of the most distinguished living scholars. Moreover, a thirst for poetical translations of the classics was now very keen with the public, who had, ten years before, welcomed Creech's *Lucretius*, and had been spurring Dryden on to further triumphs in the direction of Horace and Virgil. Everything was combined to give the young poet a fair opportunity of displaying his powers of verse and scholarship.

In the course of the seventeenth century, two industrious writers, Stapylton and Barton Holiday, had successively presented the world with English versions of Juvenal, which kept tolerably close to the original, but which lacked all the poetic graces. Oldham, that Marcellus of our satire, whom Dryden loved and had melodiously lamented, found Juvenal particularly congenial to his own profuse and violent genius, and paraphrased the third and thirteenth satires picturesquely and loosely. The version in which Congreve now took part was proposed and edited by Dryden, who had become very social in his old age, and loved to collect the young poets round him. Of the sixteen satires he undertook five himself, gave two to Nahum Tate, one to Creech, one to each of his own sons, one to young George Stepney, of Trinity College, Cambridge, and divided the rest among less-known writers. Congreve received the eleventh as his share. On the whole the performance, though the work of eleven men, is very uniform in quality, Dryden being easily and usually happiest in phrase as well as in verse. Prefixed to the collection is one of the latest, and certainly one of the fullest and most valuable of Dryden's critical essays, alone enough to give permanent value to the volume. This is dedicated, in a too fulsome strain of eulogy, to the satiric poet the Earl of Dorset, then Lord Chamberlain. Dorset was a man of uncommon talent, "the best good man with the worst-natured Muse," an easy-going creature of the most indulgent order, who amused himself, in literature, by pouring forth none but waspish sentiments. Dorset, who still holds some small place among the minor English poets, read, let us hope with a blush, that the greatest commendation Dryden's own partiality ever gave the best of his own pieces was that they were imitations of Dorset's. In a less painfully obsequious spirit Dryden presents to the Mæcenas of the day his fellow-labourers; "some of them," he says, "have the honour to be known to your Lordship already, and they who have not yet that happiness desire it now." Congreve, no doubt, was one of the latter class.

The Eleventh Satire is not one which we should select for special praise if all were anonymous, yet Congreve has done his work well. He is a little too copious in his paraphrase; he extends the 208 lines of Juvenal to nearly double that number. But in this he is not a greater sinner than his colleagues, and perhaps the entire sense of one of Juvenal's dense and full-bodied lines could not be rendered in less than a couplet. This is how Congreve translates the prettiest passage in this satire, the description of the *menu* which Persicus must expect.

> Be not surprised that 'tis all homely cheer,
> For nothing from the shambles I provide,
> But from my own small farm, the tenderest kid
> And fattest of my flock, a suckling yet,
> That ne'er had nourishment but from the teat.
> No bitter willow-tops have been its food,
> Scarce grass; its veins have more of milk than blood.
> Next that, shall mountain sparagus be laid,
> Pulled by some plain but cleanly country-maid;
> The largest eggs, yet warm within the nest,

Together with the hens that laid them, dressed;
Clusters of grapes, preserved for half a year,
Which, plump and fresh as on the vine, appear;
Apples of a rich flavour, fresh and fair,
Mixed with the Syrian and the Signian pear,—
Mellowed by winter from their cruder juice,
Light of digestion now, and fit for use.

At the close of the *Juvenal*, with a new title-page and pagination, come *The Satires of Aulus Persius Flaccus.* In this province Dryden reigns alone, having travelled unassisted through the six dark and thorny poems. But here we find Congreve, though quite unknown to the world, exalted above all his colleagues. The only complimentary poem affixed to the *Persius* is his, and this is the earliest of his notable publications. It is a fine poem of compliment from "the youngest to the oldest singer" of the age, celebrating Dryden as the heroic knight who has freed the captive Persius from the magic enchantment of his own obscurity, and who deserves the title of "great Revealer of dark Poesie." The whole poem is eloquent, inspired by genuine intellectual passion, the critical passion of the scholar and lover of literature, without expression of personal feeling or humanity of any kind, and in its dry light of wit and intelligence reveals the Congreve that we presently learn to respect and admire, but never really learn to know. He sums up his critical encomium thus:—

So stubborn flints their inward heat conceal,
Till art and force the unwilling sparks reveal,
But, through your skill, from these small seeds of fire,
Bright flames arise, which never can expire.

In an age when even the grossness of compliment was apt to fail in pleasing, this was praise given with tact, for such a result was precisely that which Dryden had hoped for. He had but little respect for the "scabrous and hobbling" muse of Persius, and was ready to be assured that his translation formed a much better poem than the original. Congreve did wisely, in praising Dryden, to emphasise his wonder that so bright a flower of poesy should spring from so poor a Latin seed.

The young Staffordshire poet had achieved a signal success in winning the affection of Dryden, to whom, it would appear, he had lately been presented. At this time Dryden was at the height of his fame. He had outlived the troubles of his early career; his enemies had fallen away, and had left him calm. The wicked Earl of Rochester was dead, and Shadwell was dying; Mulgrave had become a friend and Crowne was cowed and pacified; such insects as Elkanah Settle had had their day, had stung and had fallen. At length the great and weary Dryden was at rest, and in the time of his fame and his success, he had developed a noble magnanimity. He was by far the most eminent living English writer, and he who had fought so hard all through his youth and middle life was fighting still, but no longer with his fellow-artists. He had become a sort of good giant, and he amused himself, in his conscious kingship, by looking round to find some one to reign in poetry after him. Ten years earlier he thought he had found a successor in Oldham, but that promising young poet died on the threshold of his career. There is evidence to show that Dryden immediately and finally concluded that this young William Congreve, with his one unpolished play in his pocket, was the coming man, and he expended his confidence and his affection upon him at once.

The person who introduced the obscure young Templar to the court of Dryden is understood to have been Captain Thomas Southerne. This man had enjoyed his momentary triumph as a possible coming poet, but although he had ushered in the school of Orange dramatists, he did not attempt to retain a position which was hardly suited to his very respectable powers. He was an Irishman, and a graduate of Trinity College, but he had left Dublin before Congreve came from school. His first plays, a tragedy and a comedy, had enjoyed more success than they properly deserved. Southerne had yet to learn his art. He was taken away from the theatre to serve in the army, and rose to the grade of captain before the Revolution. When Congreve arrived in London, Southerne was just making a second start in theatrical life. There were few greater successes than his *Sir Anthony Love* enjoyed in 1691, and *The Wives' Excuse* in 1692 was almost more lucky, for though the public slighted it, the literary world, with Dryden at its head, indignantly applauded. Dryden wrote a consolatory epistle to Southerne, in which he advised him to write another comedy:—

> The standard of thy style let Etheredge be;
> For wit, the immortal spring of Wycherley;
> Learn after both to draw some just design,
> And the next age will learn to copy thine.

This was too large an order for Southerne to carry out, but we might fancy that he passed it on to his young friend Congreve. Southerne presently found his true vocation in a sentimental species of tragedy, founded upon Otway.

We learn from an expression of Cibber's that Southerne was by this time a sort of reader for the stage; and Congreve may have introduced himself to him in this capacity, with the MS. of *The Old Bachelor* in his hand; or the common training at Dublin may have brought them together at once. Southerne was ever afterwards on an intimate footing with Congreve, and forty years later supplied information, unfortunately of a partly incorrect character, regarding the early life of the latter. Other friends who are mentioned among those who early saw the merit of Congreve, and helped to recommend him to the notice of Dryden, are Walter Moyle and Arthur Maynwaring. Moyle was a brilliant Oxford man, a little younger than Congreve, and, like him, a Templar. Nothing that Moyle has left behind him can be said to justify the very high opinion of his contemporaries. Dryden spoke of "that learning and judgment, above his age, which every one discovers in Mr. Moyle." Before the close of the century he entered Parliament as member for Saltash, in his native county of Cornwall, and faded away out of literary society. His *Works*, pompously edited in 1727, consist of political tracts and translations from Greek prose; and he is remembered only in connection with Congreve.

Another truncated reputation is that of Arthur Maynwaring, who had personally interviewed the great Boileau, and was supposed to have imbibed poetical wisdom from under that mighty periwig. He also was a Templar, and he had led off with an anonymous satire so vigorously turned that the town had taken it for Dryden's. As alike the *protégé* of Congreve's father's patron, Lord Burlington, and of the English Mæcenas, Lord Dorset, Maynwaring was probably instrumental in launching Congreve on the polite world. It is particularly stated that he was engaged in 1692, in company with Southerne and Dryden, on the preparation of *The Old Bachelor* for the stage, and that he even revised it. We shall occasionally meet with the name of Maynwaring in this history, although, like Moyle, he abandoned literature for politics, and became a court-journalist and member of Parliament. He died prematurely in the year 1712. He was a man of fine judgment, brilliant conversation, and unsullied honour—asserting, in a corrupt age, the value of an absolute purity in official life.

In the company of these friends, but under what exact circumstances we shall never know, the comedy which Congreve had brought with him in his pocket from the country was gradually polished for the stage. As early as the summer of 1692, *The Old Bachelor* was not merely accepted at the Theatre Royal, but Thomas Davenant, the manager of that house, gave Congreve, six months before the performance of his piece, the then unprecedented privilege, to a new writer, of a free entrance to the theatre. Southerne records that when he showed the MS. to Dryden, that poet declared that "he never saw such a first play in his life, and that the author not being acquainted with the stage or the town, it would be a pity to have it miscarry for want of a little assistance; the stuff was rich indeed, only the fashionable cut was wanting." Southerne, Maynwaring, and Dryden united to add this last polish, and Congreve wisely let them do with his play what they would. These critics were loud in their commendations, and the young poet's vanity would have been sickly indeed, if he had not welcomed the aid which their superior knowledge of theatrical affairs afforded him.

The moment was a very trying one in the history of the stage, and when *The Old Bachelor* was finally produced in January, 1693, the actors at Theatre Royal needed the best play they could get, and the most favourable opinions, to enable them to make way against the unparalleled misfortunes of that winter. The month of December had deprived the company of three of those actors to whom, after Betterton, it mainly looked for support. On the 9th of December, 1692, the amiable and gifted William Mountfort, the most graceful and impassioned actor of young lovers' parts which the stage then possessed, was murdered in Norfolk Street, Strand, by Lord Mohun and Captain Hill, mainly, it would seem, because of the fire which he threw into his scenes with the beautiful Mrs. Bracegirdle, of whom those turbulent bloods had the impertinence to be enamoured. Within a week after this tragical event—although, this time, from natural causes—the unexpected deaths of two other leading actors, Nokes and Leigh, shocked the town. Nokes had been the most farcical of comedians, Leigh the most fantastic; and their loss left a terrible gap in the ranks of the Theatre Royal. In reading *The Old Bachelor*, we are not permitted to doubt that the part of Fondlewife was adapted, in some of its special touches, to Leigh, and that of Sir Joseph Wittol to Nokes; while Vainlove was cut out with equal obviousness for Mountfort. These unfortunate losses gave opportunity, however, for young and ambitious actors to rise to stronger characters than had yet been allotted to them; and, in particular, the Irish actor, Thomas Doggett, who had waited until then for promotion, was allowed to take the critical part of Fondlewife.

The curtain rose, and an amusing prologue was spoken by Mrs. Bracegirdle, who pretended to break down and forget her part, and finally to run away, without ever deviating from excellent heroic verse. The first act tried the endurance of the public, and proved its intellectual temper. There was no movement at all; the entire act consisted of conversation between four gentlemen in a London street, nor did there appear in the conduct of the story, as so far sketched, any freshness of invention or advance upon the comic types of Wycherley. But the wit, the sparkle, the delicate finish of the dialogue were something, till that night, unparalleled on the British stage. The language—as Macaulay puts it—was "resplendent with wit and eloquence." From all its facets the sharply-cut dialogue flashed the pure light of the diamond, and the audience, a little bewildered at first, sat amazed and respectful. When the great Betterton (in the part of Heartwell, the surly Old Bachelor himself) appeared on the stage, and supported Powell (as Bellmour), with his prestige and the magical melody of his voice, the success of the play was assured.

But the first act passed, and the first scene of the second act, without the appearance of a single actress. In this whetting of the popular expectation, however, there was a signal artifice, for as a point of fact all the female beauty and talent of the English stage were collected behind the scenes, ready to be introduced. Even the fair and comical Mrs. Mountfort, though her murdered husband was scarcely at rest in his grave, was required to take the difficult part of Belinda. By far the most pleasing figure in *The Old Bachelor*, and its only entirely innocent and virtuous character, is Araminta, whose hand is at last wasted upon the worthless Vainlove. For this part only one woman on the London stage could be thought of, namely Anne Bracegirdle, then in her thirtieth year and at the zenith of her charms. To Mrs. Bracegirdle this first performance of *The Old Bachelor* was destined to prove a momentous affair; the current of her life was permanently altered by it. So large a part does this illustrious and admirable woman take in the life of Congreve, that this seems the place to introduce her more completely in the eloquent words of Colley Cibber :—

Mrs. Bracegirdle was now [1690 or 1691] but just blooming to her maturity; her reputation as an actress gradually rising with that of her person; never any woman was in such general favour of her spectators, which, to the last scene of her dramatic life, she maintained by not being unguarded in her private character. This discretion contributed not a little to make her the *cara*, the darling of the theatre; for it will be no extravagant thing to say, scarce an audience saw her that were less than half of them lovers, without a suspected favourite among them; and though she might be said to have been the universal passion, and under the strongest temptations, her constancy in resisting them served but to increase the number of her admirers, and this perhaps you will more easily believe when I extend not my encomiums on her person beyond a sincerity that can be suspected; for she had no greater claim to beauty than what the most desirable brunette might pretend to. But her youth and lively aspect threw out such a glow of health and cheerfulness that on the stage few spectators, that were not past it, could behold her without desire. It was even a fashion among the gay and young to have a taste or *tendre* for Mrs. Bracegirdle.

According to the universal tradition of the age, this cold and discreet actress deviated from the path of discretion, if ever, only or almost only in favour of Congreve, for whom, at all events, to the day of his death, she preserved a close and affectionate friendship. It was for her that in every instance Congreve wrote the leading parts in his dramas, and he seems to have indulged his own feeling for the actress by invariably making her play the part of an admired and courted queen of beauty.

It was Doggett's acting of the ludicrous part of Fondlewife, the Puritan banker, which finally and completely conquered the house. The fourth and fifth acts, although the weakness of the latter is very obvious to the reader of *The Old Bachelor*, went in a splendid popular triumph. Davies says, in his *Dramatic Miscellanies*, that when Mrs. Barry, Mrs. Bracegirdle, Mrs. Mountfort, and Mrs. Bowman appeared together on the stage at the end, the audience fervently applauded the galaxy of their beauty. No doubt the fact is correct, except in one particular; Mrs. Barry had nothing to do on the stage in the last scene. She acted Letitia Fondlewife; but if we replace Mrs. Barry by Mrs. Leigh, the quartet is again complete. Mrs. Barry, who had but little scope for her peculiar dignity of bearing in the character of Letitia, was rewarded by speaking the epilogue. Congreve was always very adroit in the stage-distribution of his pieces.

The Old Bachelor ran for fourteen nights, an extraordinary success in those days. It was no less successful as a book; on the 23rd of March a third edition was published, and it continued to be reprinted. The original issue was dedicated to Lord Clifford, the eldest son of the Earl of Burlington, of whose Irish estates Colonel Congreve, the poet's father, had been manager at Lismore. A well-written preface confesses, as far as the critics are concerned, "that if they who find some faults in [this play] were as intimate with it as I am, they would find a great many more." But the young playwright had little to fear from the critics. Applause was universal, and came as freely from the men of letters as from the public. Southerne, charmed to find his *protégé* a success, prefixed to the printed *Old Bachelor* a magnificent tribute of recognition:—

> Dryden has long extended his command,
> By right divine, quite through the Muses' land,
> Absolute Lord; and, holding now from none
> But great Apollo his undoubted crown,—
> (That empire settled, and grown old in power,)
> Can wish for nothing but a successor,
> Not to enlarge his limits, but maintain
> Those provinces which he alone could gain.
> His eldest, Wycherley, in wise retreat,
> Thought it not worth his quiet to be great;
> Loose wandering Etheredge, in wild pleasures tost,
> And foreign interests, to his hopes long lost;

> Poor Lee and Otway dead! CONGREVE appears
> The Darling and last comfort of his years!
> May'st thou live long in thy great Master's smiles,
> And, growing under him, adorn these isles;
> But when,—when part of him (be that but late!)
> His body yielding must submit to fate,
> Leaving his deathless works, and thee, behind
> (The natural successor of his mind),
> Then may'st thou finish what he has begun,
> Heir to his merit, be in fame his son.

We may be sure that Southerne, generously waiving his own claim to the poetical succession, would not have addressed the lad of twenty-three in these exalted tones if Dryden had not given the key-note. Following on the dedication to the *Persius*, and taken with what we know of Dryden's recorded utterances a little later, we may take it for granted that the first poet of the age very openly and explicitly expressed his full belief in a splendid future for Congreve. Another congratulator, J. D. Marsh, remarked that in *The Old Bachelor* Congreve,

> Like a well-mettled hawk, took flight,
> Quite out of reach and almost out of sight,

while Bevil Higgons, in words as direct as Southerne's, predicted that the new poet would succeed Dryden, and be the glory of the coming age. A very clever but most indecent prologue was volunteered by an unknown bard, and though not spoken, was printed; it turned out to be written by Anthony, fourth Lord Falkland. Already, too, we find that Congreve's equable good-nature and fidelity in friendship had struck those who knew him. Hopkins, exiled from London, writes a letter in verse to Walter Moyle, published in 1694 in his *Epistolary Poems*, in which he breathes his pious wishes thus for his most eminent contemporaries :—

> In full delights let sprightly Southerne live,
> With all that woman and that wine can give;
> May generous Wycherley, all sufferings past,
> Enjoy a well-deserved estate at last;
> Late, very late, may the great Dryden die,
> But when deceased, may Congreve rise as high,
> To him my service and my love commend,
> The greatest wit and yet the truest friend—

and such allusions to the great new poet, not less early, are to be found elsewhere. The success of *The Old Bachelor* was the most rousing event in our literary history between the Revolution and the accession of Anne. Seldom has a new luminary appeared so vast and so splendid as its orb first slipped above the horizon.

There were many reasons, besides the exceptional combination of beauty and talent on the stage, why *The Old Bachelor* should enjoy a great success. To us who compare it, not with its predecessors, but with its three greater and younger sisters, it may appear old-fashioned and thin. Congreve was always improving, and to see how his style developed we have only to put *The Old Bachelor*, where he is still a disciple of Wycherley, beside *The Way of the World*, where he is superbly and entirely himself. But to those who sat at the Theatre Royal through that first performance in January, 1693, the effect of so modern and so brilliant a play must have been something overwhelming. The Revolution had put a slight barrier between the old theatre and the new; the Restoration dramatists, with the exception of Dryden and Shadwell, had given way to a younger school of Orange poets, not yet generally recognized. Except for Dryden's *Amphitryon* and Southerne's *Sir Anthony Love*, not the one nor the other a very startling production, comedy had gone back into the hands of Shadwell, who was now just dead, after a recent period of great dramatic activity. The plays of this unfortunate writer are not by any means contemptible, but Shadwell preserved the old coarse tradition of Restoration comedy, with its violent demarcation of character, its fantastic jargon, and its vulgarly emphatic incident. Etheredge had now been silent for twenty, and Wycherley for fifteen years. No one had arisen who had accepted the principles of these great fathers of our modern comedy, and it seemed as though they had written in vain. Dryden never contrived to catch the secret of this Gallic lightness; Crowne had secured something of it once, in his *Sir Courtly Nice*, only to lose it again immediately. In *The Old Bachelor* it came back once more, and in a hand that was as much firmer than Etheredge's as it was subtler and tenderer than Wycherley's. The faults of the play were due to the inexperience or timidity of the writer. The merits were such as justified to the full the enthusiasm of the age.

When Steele came to criticise *The Old Bachelor* in *The Tatler*, he specially praised the distinction of the characters. In Wycherley's comedies everybody had been brutally witty all round; ladies had talked like rakes, and footmen had made similes. It would be interesting to know how far, in making this advance, Congreve had wittingly gone to school with Molière. In Wycherley's drama not only the great French comedian, but Racine also, in his *Plaideurs*, had been laid under contribution. Manly and Olivia owed much to their freer and more human prototypes, Alceste and Célimène, and *The Country Wife* directly recalls *L'École des Femmes*. In *The Old Bachelor* there is no positive evidence of the study of Molière, whom Congreve, who read so much, must nevertheless have known familiarly, but the direct influence of Wycherley is strongly marked. Hartwell is only the Plain Dealer in another form; Fondlewife, in certain aspects, had already appeared as Gripe in *Love in a Wood*, and as Pinchwife in *The Country Wife*. Wittol and Bluff are as old as comedy itself; they are fine old crusted stage properties, and we need take no trouble to discover their originals. This absence of novelty in the arrangement of the characters makes it the more interesting that, as Steele says, they are so strongly and carefully distinguished.

We read *The Old Bachelor* with interest, and return to it with pleasure, but to the critic its main attraction is that it marks the transition between the imitation of Wycherley and Congreve's complete confidence in his own powers. It contains some admirable single scenes. The first in the second act, where Sharper persuades Sir Joseph Wittol to pay him one hundred pounds for an imaginary service is of the very first order. The character of Vainlove, "one of Love's April fools," with his cynical sensibility, is brought into excellent contrast with the peevish frivolity of Belinda, and wins, without deserving it, the steady affection of Araminta. The Fondlewife and Letitia business has become too distressing for any conceivable audience to endure, but is carried on with the utmost vivacity and impudence. It has to be admitted, on the other hand, that the fragments of the play do not coalesce, that the perfection of the language very imperfectly conceals or clothes the brutality of the sentiments, and that we are only too well prepared for the moral with which the fifth act closes:—

> What rugged ways attend the noon of life!
> Our sun declines, and with what anxious strife,
> What pain, we tug that galling load a Wife.

Every artifice was introduced to make *The Old Bachelor* popular—dances, pantomime, a song and violins. The song, "Thus to a ripe consenting maid," is one of Congreve's best.

Malone suggested that the song which Congreve contributed to Southerne's comedy of *The Maid's Last Prayer* was probably "the first acknowledged essay presented by Congreve to the public." The *Persius*, *The Old Bachelor*, and Southerne's play appeared with the same date, 1693, on the title-page of each, and Malone did not know which came first. But from the *London Gazette* we learn that *The Maid's Last Prayer* was published on the 9th of March, 1693, and therefore followed *The Old Bachelor* by at least six weeks. The song occurs in the fifth act, and is a very typical example of Congreve's satirical observation of the female heart:—

> Tell me no more I am deceived,
> That Chloë's false and common;

By Heaven ! I all along believed
  She was a very woman ;
As such I liked, as such caressed,
She still was constant,—when possessed,
  She could do more for no man.

But oh ! her thoughts on others ran,
  And that you think a hard thing?
Perhaps she fancied you the man?
  Why, what care I one farthing?
You think she's false, I'm sure she's kind,
I'll take her body, you her mind.
  Who has the better bargain?

This song was set to music by Henry Purcell and sung by Mrs. Ayliffe. As there is no record of any other instance in which the great Purcell, who died two years later, collaborated with Congreve, it is probably to this time that must be attributed a story preserved in Benjamin Victor's *Epistle to Sir Richard Steele*, published in 1722, when Congreve and Dennis were both still alive. It runs thus :—

Mr. Purcell and Mr. Congreve, going into a tavern, by chance met D——s, who went in with 'em ; after a glass or two has passed, Mr. Purcell, having some private business with Mr. Congreve, wanted D——s out of the room, and not knowing a more certain way than punning, (for you are to understand, Sir, Mr. D——s is as much surprised at [a] Pun as at a Bailiff,) he proceeded after the following manner. He pulled at the bell, and called two or three times, but no one answering, he put his hand under the table, and looking full at D——s, he said, "I think this table is like the Tavern." Says D——s (with his usual profane phrase), "God's death ! Sir, how is this table like the tavern?" "Why," says Mr. Purcell, "because here's ne'er a drawer in it." Says D——s, starting up, "Sir, the man that will make such an execrable pun as that in my company, will pick my pocket," and so left the room.

The retort is well known, and has commonly been attributed to Dr. Johnson.

CHAPTER II.

THE success of *The Old Bachelor* raised Congreve at the age of twenty-three to the first rank among contemporary poets. He was helped to support his amazing literary triumph by the accidental advantages which nature had showered upon him. His person was singularly beautiful, he was an athlete until fast living consumed his constitution, and although indolent, he was so gracious and so sympathetic that he pleased without effort, and conquered the esteem of those who might have envied a popularity less indifferently borne. Dryden, as tradition tells us, liked him from the first, and as we descend the year 1693 we discover various records of his preference. In July, in his preface to the *Third Miscellany*, he brought Congreve's name forward, and added that he was one "whom I cannot mention without the honour which is due to his excellent parts, and that entire affection which I bear him." To this same *Third Miscellany* Congreve contributed a fragment of translated Homer, the lamentation of Priam on the body of Hector. He is known to have been an admirable scholar, and Dryden desired him to undertake a complete version of the *Iliad*. Had he done so, Pope's translation would probably have never seen the light, but Congreve was too indolent for the execution of so extended a task. His longest flight in this direction was taken later on when he rendered into heroics the *Hymn to Venus*. In August, writing to Jacob Tonson from Northamptonshire, Dryden sends a message to no other London friend, yet adds: "I am Mr. Congreve's true lover, and desire you to tell him how kindly I take his often remembrances of me. I wish him all prosperity, and hope I shall never lose his affection."

Macaulay has positively stated, and Thackeray has inferred, that immediately after the production of *The Old Bachelor*, Montague gave Congreve a place in the Civil Service. Thackeray adds: "Doesn't it sound like a fable, that place in the Pipe Office?" If not exactly a fable, it is at least a fact that rests on insufficient evidence. It is founded, so far as I can discover, on the article in the *Biographia Britannica*, to which certain notes by Southerne give a peculiar air of veracity. This article says, that early in 1693, "Charles Montague, Lord Halifax, being desirous to place so eminent a wit in a state of ease and tranquillity, made him *immediately* one of the Commissioners for licensing hackney-coaches, bestowed upon him soon after a place in the Pipe Office, and gave him likewise a post in the Custom House of the value of six hundred pounds a year." There is probably some error here, so far as the word "immediately" is concerned. In the first place, it is perhaps frivolous to remark that Charles Montague did not become Lord Halifax until December, 1700; but it is to the point to notice that he was not made Chancellor of the Exchequer, and was not therefore in a position to scatter gifts of place, until the summer of 1694. In the dedication to *The Double Dealer*, moreover, Congreve seems to acknowledge, for the present at all events, none but literary favours. Montague has read and criticized his play, and he handsomely thanks him. If more material favours had at this time been shown, the poet must have expressed his gratitude in other terms. Finally, in a late poem of Swift's we read :—

> Thus Congreve spent in writing plays,
> And one poor office, half his days;
> While Montague, who claimed the station
> To be Mæcenas to the nation,
> For poets open table kept,
> But ne'er considered where they slept ;
> Himself as rich as fifty Jews,
> Was easy, though they wanted shoes,
> And crazy Congreve scarce could spare
> A shilling to discharge his chair.

"Crazy" means feeble, invalided ; and therefore cannot refer to a time when Congreve was in the flush of youth and health ; while "half his days," if roughly calculated, brings us at earliest to 1700. On the whole, it seems improbable that he was in possession of any pluralities of office in these early days. He had some private fortune, and his literary work was lucrative and tolerably ample. The sale of his plays alone must have been a source of considerable income. Until further evidence is forthcoming we must hesitate to accept the common view of Congreve as all through his life a holder of fat sinecures.

He was not long in preparing a second comedy. Early

in November, 1693, *The Double Dealer* was produced at the Theatre Royal. In a letter to Walsh, Dryden records the comparative failure of this play. He says: "Congreve's *Double Dealer* is much censured by the greater part of the town, and is defended only by the best judges, who, you know, are commonly the fewest. Yet it gains ground daily, and has already been acted eight times." The reasons for this want of fortune are not far to seek. "The gentlemen were offended with him for the discovery of their follies," and, in particular, it would seem, for the exposure of the hateful practice of making personal friendship, without further excuse, a mask for taking a dishonourable advantage in love. It is this crime against which *The Double Dealer* is a satire, and so far the moral purpose of Congreve seems praiseworthy. But the heartless treachery of Maskwell, who is one of the most appalling scoundrels in imaginative literature, is overdone. He is a devil, pure and simple, and not a man at all. When his skein of villanies is all unwound, we feel inclined to cry, with Lord Touchwood, "I am confounded when I look back, and want a clue to guide me through the various mazes of unheard-of treachery." Congreve was in the right when he objected to the stupid way in which his satire had been received, but perhaps he hardly realized what slaps he had given to the faces of his audience. That he was very angry the epistle dedicatory of his first edition shows. He retained part of this well-written address to Montague, but as his temper cooled he omitted the worst which he had said in his wrath. It may be interesting to resuscitate the most important of these omissions:—

And give me leave, without any flattery to you, or vanity in myself, to tell my illiterate critics, as an answer to their impotent objections, that they have found fault with that which has been pleasing to you. This play, in relation to my concern for its reputation, succeeded before it was acted, for through your early patronage, it had an audience of several persons of the first rank both in wit and quality; and their allowance of it was a consequence of your approbation. Therefore if I really wish it might have had a more popular reception, it is not at all in consideration of myself, but because I wish well, and would gladly contribute to, the benefit of the stage and diversion of the town. They were not long since so kind to a very imperfect comedy of mine that I thought myself justly indebted to them all my endeavours for an entertainment that might merit some little of that applause which they were so lavish of when I thought I had no title to it. But I find they are to be treated cheaply, and I have been at an unnecessary expense.

It is never wise to scold like this; and here is something even worse :—

I hear a great many of the fools are angry at me, and I am glad of it, for I writ at them, not to them. This is a bold confession, and yet I don't think I shall disoblige one person by it, for nobody can take it to himself, without owning the character.

The fact was that after drinking a cup of unexampled sweetness, Congreve was now tasting the first bitter drop of inevitable reaction. For biographical purposes we have restored these evidences of his momentary petulance, but let it not be forgotten that he himself immediately suppressed them.

The cast was a strong one; indeed, one would have supposed, even stronger than that of *The Old Bachelor*. Betterton gave the force of his robust genius to the detestable character of Maskwell, Doggett had a good opportunity for his farcical vivacity in Sir Paul Plyant, there were all the lovely ladies, the Bracegirdle, the Barry, the Mountfort, the Leigh. In addition to these, Kynaston, with his amazing beauty still unimpaired in old age, reminded the spectators by his Lord Touchwood of that charm and bloom of youth which had graced so many women's parts at the beginning of the reign of Charles II. But probably Williams was not quite strong enough to carry him well through the trying situations in which the hero,—if hero he be,—Mellefont, is constantly placed by his trusting disposition. From what we gather, it would seem to have been the incredulity of the audience in Mellefont which nearly wrecked the comedy.

But there was something worse than this. The ladies were angry, as Dryden told Walsh, and to see why they were angry needs no very great penetration. As is well known, ladies came in masks to the first night of Restoration and Orange comedies. They had good need to do so, since free as the discourse may have been at their own firesides, it was far outdone on the cynical and shameless stage. The dramatists had again and again drawn attention, especially in their prologues and epilogues, to the difficulty of distinguishing virtue from vice when each wore a vizard. But no one had carried his satire so far, or had pushed it home so keenly and so adroitly as Congreve in the third act of the *The Double Dealer*. "I find women," his Careless had said, "are not the same bare-faced and in masks, and a vizor disguises their inclinations as much as their faces." And Mellefont, the man of virtue and honour, had replied, "'Tis a mistake, for women may most properly be said to be unmasked when they wear vizors, for that secures them from blushing, and being out of countenance, and next to being in the dark, or alone, they are most truly themselves in a vizor-mask." The galleries "where," as Crowne puts it, "roosting masques sat cackling for a mate," must have thrilled with indignation at such audacity. The poet told them, when they complained, that they should no more expect to be complimented in a comedy than tickled by the surgeon when they went to be bled. The position was a bold one, and Congreve dared to sustain it. It probably accounts for his ultimate failure to please the public and the ladies, although he delighted the lettered world so constantly.

A third reason assigned for the want of success of *The Double Dealer* is of more literary interest. It is said that the audience resented the frequent soliloquies by which Maskwell explained to them his intentions and the progress of the intrigue. It is curious to find Congreve making use of this artifice, because it seems to take him back directly to the study of Molière. The English comic writers eschewed soliloquy very carefully. Wycherley never, so far as I remember, leaves a single character alone upon the stage, and the theatre of Shadwell habitually swarms like an ant-hill. On the other hand, in several of Molière's comedies, the central personage of the intrigue explains his purpose to the audience in an aside, exactly in Congreve's way. George Dandin is an example, and, in *L'Amour Médecin* Sganarelle. In *L'Étourdi*, and still more in *Le Dépit Amoureux* soliloquies of Mascarille may almost be said to tie the loose members of those plays together. Congreve thought it needful to excuse his return to this old conventional practice, and said, very justly, that "we ought not to imagine that this man either talks to us, or to himself; he is only thinking, and thinking such matter as it were inexcusable folly in him to speak. But because we are concealed spectators of the plot in agitation, and the Poet finds it necessary to let us know the whole mystery of his contrivance, he is willing to inform us of this person's thoughts, and to that end is forced to make use of the expedient of speech, no other better way being yet invented for the communication of thought." Notwithstanding these ingenious arguments, Congreve managed to do without soliloquy in his next comedy, though he was obliged to return to it in *The Way of the World.* His plays were never really well-made, in the modern sense, but no more are those of Molière or Shakespeare.

In his dedication to *The Double Dealer* Congreve rather rashly asserts that he does not know that he has "borrowed one hint of it anywhere." The general design, however, with its five acts' triumph of a social impostor, has some vague analogy with *Tartuffe*, and there are three prominent scenes in which Congreve certainly followed, perhaps with conscious rivalry, in the steps of his predecessors. The criticism of acquaintances in the third act is obviously reminiscent of the scene in Olivia's chamber in *The Plain Dealer*, but it is in every respect superior. The brutality and heartlessness of Wycherley's heroine are simply shocking, while Congreve retains our sympathies and shows his superior tact by making Cynthia disgusted at the spite of Brisk and Lord Froth. Sheridan, long afterwards, in essaying to produce the same effect, made no advance upon the wit of Congreve.

It will perhaps be less generally conceded that in competing with Molière in the absurd blue-stocking scene between Lady Froth and Brisk, and in the criticism of her ladyship's remarkable lyric, the English poet has the advantage. The conversation between Oronte and Philinte, with Alceste growling in the background, the fatuity of the "petits vers doux, tendres et langoureux," the insight into the vanity of the amateur,—these are delicious in the *Misanthrope* and of a very high order of writing. But Molière—dare we say it?—prolongs the scene a little too far; the episode threaten to become wearisome to all but literary spectators; whereas the brief and ludicrous exchange of compliments between Brisk and Lady Froth is soon over, the coachman-poem is in itself more funny than "L'Espoir," and the whole incident, as it seems to me, is treated in a more laughable, and dramatically in a more legitimate, way by Congreve than by Molière. It may be added that this central portion of the third act is unquestionably the best part of the play, some of which is not quite written up to its author's mark.

There is yet a third instance in which Congreve, in spite of his claim to originality, must be held to have undergone the influence of a predecessor. When Lady Plyant pays her monstrous attentions to Mellefont, it is impossible to avoid a comparison with the advances Bélise makes to Clitandre in the first act of *Les Femmes*

Savantes. This is what reminded Macaulay of the house of Laius or of Pelops, and no one will deny its horror. But in sheer wit and intellectual daring, the English dialogue does not seem to me to be at all inferior to the French.

The Double Dealer contains some excellent characters. Sir Paul Plyant, with his night-cap made out of a piece of a scarlet petticoat, tied up in bed, out of harm's way, and looking, with his great beard, like a Russian bear upon a drift of snow, is wholly delightful; and Lady Froth, the charming young blue-stocking, with her wit and her pedantry, her affectation and her merry vitality, is one of the best and most complex characters that Congreve has created. Her doting affection for her child, "poor little Sappho," mingled with her interest in her own ridiculous verses, and set off by her genuine ability and power, combine to form a very life-like picture. Twenty years earlier she might have been supposed to be a study of Margaret, Duchess of Newcastle. Her astronomical experiments with Mr. Brisk are a concession on the poet's part to the worst instincts of his audience, and funny as they undeniably are, they spoil the part.

A fault in the construction of *The Double Dealer* is that Lord and Lady Froth are not sharply enough distinguished from Lord and Lady Touchwood. In Cynthia, Congreve produced one of those gracious and honest maidens whom he liked to preserve in the wild satiric garden of his drama, that his beloved Mrs. Bracegirdle might have a pure and impassioned part to play. We owe to this penchant the fortunate circumstance that, while in Etheredge, Wycherley, and Vanbrugh there is often not a single character that we can esteem or personally tolerate from the beginning of the play to the end, in Congreve there is always sure to be one lady of reputation, even if she be not quite of the crystalline order of that more famous Lady, who walked among apes and tigers in the boskages of *Comus*.

The Double Dealer was published on the 4th of December, 1693,[1] with the date 1694 on the title-page. Every part of the publication breathed defiance. The motto on the title was "Interdum tamen, et vocem comædia tollit," and the new Chremes raged in the dedication to Montague, of which mention has already been made. Moreover, in large italic type, an epistle "To my dear Friend Mr. Congreve," displayed the scorn and anger of Dryden at this new exhibition of public tastelessness. This poem, in seventy-seven of Dryden's most muscular verses, sealed Congreve with the stamp of immortality. Perhaps since the beginning of literary history there is no other example of such full and generous praise of a young colleague by a great old poet. Dryden goes back to "the giant race before the flood," the race of Elizabeth, who wrote magnificently by instinct, ignoring the rules of art. Then came Charles II., and his poets, who cultivated verse-making, and of whom Dryden himself was chief; "but what we gained in skill we lost in strength." The architectonics of post-Restoration poetry had lacked something, in spite of the science of the builders,

[1] "London Gazette."

Till you, the best Vitruvius, come at length,
Our beauties equal, but excel our strength;
Firm Doric pillars found your solid base,
The fair Corinthian crowns the higher space,
Thus all below is strength and all above is grace.

Fletcher was master of easy dialogue, he says, and Jonson had all that judgment could give; Congreve excels them both, the first in wit, the second in learning. Etheredge, Wycherley, and Southerne have started modern comedy, but all rejoice to see Congreve lightly pass them, "ravis," as Racine would say, "d'être vaincus dans leur propre science;"

All this in blooming youth you have achieved,
Nor are your foiled contemporaries grieved,
So much the sweetness of your manners move,
We cannot envy you, because we love.

After bringing his survey of our dramatic literature to a close with a characteristic flout at the dead Shadwell and the living Rymer, Dryden proceeds to bequeath his own crown of bays to Congreve:—

And this I prophecy,—thou shalt be seen
(Though with some short parenthesis between)
High on the throne of wit, and, seated there,
Not mine (that's little), but thy laurel wear.
Thy first attempt an early promise made,
That early promise this has more than paid;
So bold, yet so judiciously you dare,
That your least praise is to be regular;

> Time, place and action may with pains be wrought,
> But genius must be born, and never can be taught:
> This is your portion, this your native store;
> Heaven that but once was prodigal before,
> To Shakespeare gave as much, she could not give *him* more.

Dryden proceeds, after this sumptuous eulogy, to refer in pathetic numbers to his own condition; he is already worn with cares and age, and just abandoning the ungrateful stage, but he foresees that Congreve is born to better fortune, and in reflecting on his own end, he breaks out into these poignant and justly celebrated lines:—

> Be kind to my remains; and oh! defend,
> Against your judgment, your departed friend!
> Let not the insulting foe my fame pursue,
> But shade those laurels which descend to you.

We shall see later on that Congreve showed by his fidelity to Dryden's reputation that he deserved the confidence so tenderly reposed in him.

It was the singular good fortune of this unsuccessful comedy to call forth in its defence, not merely the greatest poet of the existing age, but the leading genius of the next. In November, and before Queen Mary's visit turned the tide in favour of *The Double Dealer*, Swift had addressed to Congreve a long epistle, extending to more than two hundred lines. Three times before, he says, he had tried to write his friend a poem, but in vain; the rhymes refused to come. On this slightly more propitious occasion they flowed, it is plain, uneasily and awkwardly. It is curious to contrast the vigour of the thoughts and the strength of character they displayed, with the clumsy and often scarcely intelligible form. Swift was no poet, and with unusual modesty he admits it himself. "No power," he says, "beneath divine could leap the bonds which part your world and mine," that is, the worlds of the poet and the poetaster. His praise of Congreve is not more stinted than Dryden's ;

> For never did poetic mind before
> Produce a richer vein, or clearer ore,

he says, and asserts

> God-like the force of my young Congreve's bays.

It is disappointing to feel that Swift on this occasion might have, and yet did not give us any personal account of his friend. But he says, that a young spark from Farnham, who has been up to town, has brought back a rumour that Congreve talks of writing an heroic tragedy. This looks as though *The Mourning Bride* was on the stocks so early as November, 1693. This lad from Farnham speaks of "Wycherley and you and Mr. Bays," that is, Dryden, as the three first poets of the day, and arbiters of taste at Will's; so that Congreve was by this time openly recognized as Crown Prince in the Empire of literature.

It was Queen Mary's visit to *The Double Dealer* which led to a somewhat remarkable event in theatrical history. It so happened that on that afternoon Kynaston was too ill to play the part of Lord Touchwood. There was hanging about the Theatre Royal a young man of great ambition, who had been an actor since 1689, but who had hitherto found no chance of distinguishing himself. He had, however, attracted Congreve's attention, and in the embarrassing circumstances described, the poet recommended that the vacant part should be entrusted to Colley Cibber. The latter describes his rapture in the *Apology*, but his memory played him false in a detail, for he quotes, as spoken on that occasion, certain words which were specially written for a latter performance, that of the revival of *The Old Bachelor*. His own point was that his position as an actor was secured; he played Lord Touchwood extremely well, and Congreve very handsomely came round to him afterwards and told him that he had exceeded his expectations, and that he should recommend him to the Patentees. He was as good as his word, and Cibber's salary was forthwith raised from fifteen to twenty shillings a week. But Kynaston came back, there was no vacancy in the ranks, and Cibber had to wait a while longer before he took the place he longed for as *jeune premier*.

The year 1694 is almost a blank in the history of our poet. Queen Mary had been so much pleased with *The Double Dealer*, that she ordered the revival of *The Old Bachelor*, which she had not seen. Congreve wrote for the occasion a special prologue of a more business-like than strictly poetical character, pointing out how advantageous it would be for the dramatists if royalty would take the trouble to visit the theatre a little less seldom. His silence, with this exception, throughout the year is perhaps accounted for to some extent by an "epigram" in Gildon's *Chorus Poetarum*, 1694, "on the late sickness of Madam Mohun and Mr. Congreve"—

> One fatal day a sympathetic fire
> Seized him that wrote and her that did inspire,
> Mohun, the Muses' theme, their master Congreve,
> Beauty and wit, had like to have lain in one grave.

This Madam Mohun, probably, was the wife of Major Mohun, the tragic actor.

Another name was now added to the illustrious bead-roll of Congreve's friends. He became acquainted with a very brilliant young bachelor of Magdalen College, Oxford, Mr. Joseph Addison, already celebrated for his proficiency in Latin verses. Long afterwards, when he came to dedicate *The Drummer* to Congreve, in 1722, Steele said that it was Congreve who started Addison in public life, by being the instrument of his acquaintance with Montague. It was probably in return for this courtesy that Addison, addressing on the 3rd of April, 1694, his *Account of the Greatest English Poets* to Henry Sacherevell, congratulated Dryden on his successor in these terms:—

> How might we fear our English poetry,
> That long had flourished, should decay with thee,
> Did not the Muses' other hope appear,
> Harmonious Congreve, and forbid our fear;
> CONGREVE! whose fancy's unexhausted store
> Has given already much, and promised more.
> Congreve shall still preserve thy fame alive,
> And Dryden's Muse shall in his friend survive.

The closing lines of the poem referred to Addison's

intention of taking orders. It appears to have been Congreve, who, perceiving the young man's integrity and business capacity, advised Montague to make "warm instances" to Dr. Lancaster to preserve Addison as a layman. The result of this interference was, as everybody knows, eminently beneficial to Addison's fortunes. It should be noted that when Steele, thirty years later, desired to reprove Tickell for what he conceived to be a misrepresentation of Addison's early motives, it was to Congreve, as then the oldest of his intimate surviving friends, to whom he addressed his appeal.

During the year 1694 the theatrical world of London was painfully disturbed by the breaking out of that civil war at Drury Lane which threatened at one time to leave us entirely without a stage. For four years the united Patentees of the Theatre Royal had suffered no rivalry of any kind; they had enjoyed a monopoly, and they had been so anxious to swell their own dividends, that they had reduced the actors to very miserable salaries. As a matter of fact, however, their own receipts had become insufficient to keep them out of debt, since every one connected with the theatre had, it appears from what Cibber tells us, embarked on that extraordinary enterprise of Betterton's, that Indian argosy which was intended to make nabobs of the whole company at Drury Lane, and which so ignominiously fell into the hands of the French at the mouth of the English Channel in 1692. It was partly to revenge themselves for having been drawn into this misfortune and partly to lessen the prestige of the great actor, that the Patentees now began, in a very arbitrary way, to take from Betterton some of his most famous leading parts, and give them to young actors, whom they paid no better for such promotion. The direct result of this was that the audiences began to fall off. In vain the Patentees endeavoured to excite curiosity by such operas as Dryden's *King Arthur* and Betterton's *Prophetess*. In vain they produced, in 1694, so very taking a tragedy as Southerne's *Fatal Marriage*. Nothing would galvanize the dying theatre, which the loss of Mountfort, Leigh, and Nokes had seriously injured; the public became aware of the internal dissensions between actors and Patentees; and the dead-lock had cost the theatre a thousand pounds before Christmas came.

At last the actors combined to lay their grievances before Lord Dorset, the poet, who was then Lord Chamberlain. He consulted the legal advisers of the Government and received from them an opinion "that no patent for acting plays, etc., could tie up the hands of a succeeding prince, from granting the like authority, where it might be proper to trust." In other words, it was decided that the king might destroy the monopoly of Drury Lane. While Betterton and his friends, elated by this discovery, were hoping to push their scheme forward, they received a temporary check in the death of Queen Mary, which happened on the December 28, 1694. This event plunged England into mourning, and gave the minor poets an unrivalled opportunity for lyric grief. During the months of January and February a shoal of blank folio pamphlets, all with a deep black border round their title-pages, issued from the press, signed by the pens of Steele, Gould, Tate, D'Urfey, Walsh, Stepney,

Dennis, the Duke of Devonshire, and Sam Wesley, to mention no others. The death of the Archbishop of Canterbury having occurred about the same time, some of the funeral harps sounded melodiously a double woe. Dryden was silent on this occasion; but Congreve published, on January 28, 1695,[1] a sort of elegiac pastoral, entitled *The Mourning Muse of Alexis*, for which, as Luttrel tells us, his Majesty ordered that he should be paid one hundred pounds. This is the poem which Johnson so violently styled "a despicable effusion; a composition in which all is unnatural, and yet nothing is new." Nor has it found a single modern friend, except, oddly enough, a French critic, M. de Grisy, who styles the poem "sensible et presque touchant," and describes it as an interesting introduction to *The Mourning Bride*.

It is dangerous to follow Dr. Johnson in his estimates of poetry, and one reason, at least, why he objected so strongly to *The Mourning Muse of Alexis* is that it takes its inspiration, such as it is, from Spenser. Congreve invokes Virgil, and in default of the Mantuan, he calls on Spenser and Sidney. His poem is a dialogue between two shepherds, Alexis and Menalcas, and the latter remarks to the former, in the shadow of some cavern :—

> For fragrant myrtle and the blushing rose,
> Here baleful yew and deadly cypress grows ;
> Here then extended on this withered moss,
> We'll lie, and thou shalt sing of Albion's loss ;
> Of Albion's loss, and of Pastora's death,
> Begin thy mournful song, and raise thy tuneful breath.

The piece is smooth and musical, but full of vapid

[1] "London Gazette."

conceits; the flocks can graze now Queen Mary is dead, when she was alive they grew hungry by gazing on her face; the vault in which her body lies has oozy walls, and the poet, therefore, calls it a crocodile for pretending to lament its prey; Queen Mary was tall, and Congreve thinks it clever to say that she excelled all other nymphs in stature as the lofty pine o'ertops the reed. Swans, "sickening swans," are exhorted to leave their rivers, and hasten to die at her tomb, that their swan-song may be her elegy. And it all closes with this elegant alexandrian extravagance :—

> But see, Menalcas, where a sudden light
> With wonder stops my song, and strikes my sight,
> And where Pastora lies it spreads around,
> Showing all radiant bright the sacred ground,
> While from her tomb behold a flame ascends
> Of whitest fire, whose flight to heaven extends;
> On flakey wings it mounts, and quick as sight
> Cuts through the yielding air with rays of light,
> Till the blue firmament at last it gains,
> And, fixing there, a glorious star remains;
> Fairest it shines of all that light the skies,
> As once on earth were seen Pastora's eyes.

Strange that the wittiest writer of the age should be blind to the fatuity of lines that he ought to have reserved for the portfolio of Lady Froth!

The obsequies of Pastora only interrupted for a while the critical division at Drury Lane. Early in 1695, Betterton and the principal actors had an interview with William III., and were received by him with a great deal of kindness. He graciously empowered them, by a special royal license, to act elsewhere than in the Theatre

Royal in Drury Lane. This was a very important concession, and one which rendered Betterton independent of the Patentees. The next thing was to raise by private subscription, in shares of forty guineas and twenty guineas respectively, enough money to build a new theatre within the walls of the tennis-court of Lincoln's Inn Fields. The Patentees meanwhile, by promises of increased salaries, had caused a certain number of the actors to desert Betterton. Among these were Kynaston, Powell and Penkethman, while Colley Cibber and Verbruggen came into a prominence which they had never before enjoyed. The ladies, on the other hand, were extremely staunch. Early in the fray Mrs. Bracegirdle had nobly refused to take any of Mrs. Barry's parts, and the Patentees were thrown entirely upon actresses whom the public did not recognize. In their despair they had closed the Theatre Royal altogether, and from Christmas, 1694, to Easter, 1695, it would seem that London was entirely destitute of dramatic representation. On Easter Monday, however, the Patentees reopened with a revival of Mrs. Aphra Behn's *Abdelazar*, an unlucky choice, one would imagine. On the first afternoon, Cibber tells us, the house was very full, but whether it was the play or the actors that were not approved, the audience next day had sunk to nothing. Meanwhile, the process of building was going on merrily in the Lincoln's Inn tennis-court, and on the 30th of April the new rival house was opened with a fresh comedy by Congreve.

This play, *Love for Love*, had been finished in 1694, had been read and accepted by the Patentees, and only narrowly had escaped being acted perforce at Drury Lane.

Fortunately, the split between Betterton and the Patentees began to take alarming proportions before the articles of agreement were signed, and Congreve was astute enough to pause, and to see, before signing, what the event of the quarrel would be. The result was one in the highest degree beneficial to Betterton's company, for Congreve was now, without a rival, at the head of English dramatic artists. In order to secure the aid and sympathy of so valuable an ally, the management of Lincoln's Inn Theatre offered Congreve a share in their profits, on similar terms to those offered long before by the King's Company to Dryden, namely, that he should write exclusively for them. He pledged himself, "if his health permitted," to give them one new play every year. This parenthetical clause shows that already, at the age of twenty-five, the life of the tavern and the coffee-house was beginning to tell on the poet's constitution. It is scarcely needful to say that he did not carry out his engagement. He produced two more plays, at intervals of three years, and then contributed nothing more to the regular stage.

At the very outset, and while *Love for Love* was in rehearsal, an incident occurred which endangered the future of the play and of the house. Mrs. Mountfort, who was one of the most valuable actresses of the hour, whose vivacity and activity combined to make her an inimitable humourist and the very nonpareil of Miss Prues, threw up her part, because she was not allowed to be an equal sharer with the rest in the profits of the new concern. Williams, a young actor of respectable gifts, joined her in this mutiny, for the same cause, and just before the performance opened these persons seceded to the Theatre Royal. We owe to Colley Cibber the explanation, which no commentator of a later age could have supplied, that this desertion is referred to by Congreve in the prologue to *Love for Love*, when he says, congratulating the actors on their new theatre being an Eden—

> But since in Paradise frail flesh gave way,
> And when but two were made, both went astray,
> Forbear your wonder, and the fault forgive,
> If in our larger family we grieve
> One falling Adam and one tempted Eve.

This entire prologue is full of references which must have interested the audience, allusions to the burning questions of the stage, and small congratulatory confessions.

The cast, although in certain respects impoverished, was strengthened with some good new blood. In particular, Underhill, whose playing of Sir Sampson Legend always remained one of his famous parts, was a genuine acquisition. He was famous for making up a dull and mulish face of paternal perversity which threw the spectators into fits of mirth, and one of the greatest successes of *Love for Love* was the scene in which he bantered Foresight on his astrological attainments. Foresight, one of the quaintest and most original characters ever placed on the stage, was played by Sandford, another great acquisition, famous for his rendering of violent and grotesque parts, an actor whose ugliness and physical deformity made it absolutely requisite that he should personate crime or folly. Ben Legend, the sailor, was created as a part by Dogget, who attained such an extraordinary distinction in this novel character that in due time he lost his head with vanity, and about a year afterwards went over to the Patentees again, merely because he was so inflated with the sense of his own importance that he could not be satisfied with anything short of the best *rôles* on every occasion. We hear less that is definite about the mark made by the rest, although Mrs. Bracegirdle is known to have been divine in Angelica. It is difficult not to suppose that Betterton was now a little too old and heavy for Valentine, but if, as seems possible, Betterton was more like Delaunay than like any other actor whom we have seen in this generation, we can imagine that he might still, at sixty, make a very passable young philosophic spark. The inimitable sisters, Frail and Foresight, were taken by Mrs. Barry and Mrs. Bowman.

The comedy of *Love for Love* has been commonly accounted Congreve's masterpiece, and perhaps with justice. It is not quite so uniformly brilliant in style as *The Way of the World*, but it has the advantage of possessing a much wholesomer relation to humanity than that play, which is almost undiluted satire, and a more theatrical arrangement of scenes. In *Love for Love* the qualities which had shown themselves in *The Old Bachelor* and *The Double Dealer* recur, but in a much stronger degree. The sentiments are more unexpected, the language is more picturesque, the characters have more activity of mind and vitality of nature. All that was merely pink has deepened into scarlet; even what is disagreeable,—the crudity of allusion and the indecency of phrase,—have increased. The style in all its parts and qualities has become more vivid. We are looking through the same telescope as before, but the sight is better adjusted, the outlines are more definite, and the colours more intense. So wonderfully felicitous is the phraseology that we cannot doubt that if Congreve could only have kept himself unspotted from the sins of the age, dozens of tags would have passed, like bits of Shakespeare, Pope, and Gray, into habitual parlance. In spite of its errors against decency, *Love for Love* survived on the stage for more than a century, long after the remainder of Restoration and Orange drama was well-nigh extinct. Hazlitt saw it played, and thus describes it:—

> It still acts, and is still acted well. The effect of it is prodigious on the well-informed spectator. In particular, Munden's Foresight, if it is not just the thing, is a wonderfully rich and powerful piece of comic acting. His look is planet-struck; his dress and appearance like one of the signs of the zodiac taken down. Nothing can be more bewildered; and it only wants a little more helplessness, a little more of the doting, querulous, garullity of age, to be all that one conceives of the superannuated, star-gazing original.

The plot of *Love for Love* forms more interesting a story than is usually the case with Congreve. His two first plays had possessed no plot at all, properly speaking, but only in the one case a set of amatory scenes, and in the other a series of satirical situations. The hero of *Love for Love*, Valentine Legend, is a young Cambridge man, a scholar, one who loves Plato and Epictetus, but who loves pleasure also, and who, partly out of pique because Angelica, the beautiful heiress, will not marry him, has wasted all his fortune, and is reduced to the husks of a prodigal son. When the play opens he is attended in his poor lodging by his servant Jeremy, a quaint and witty fellow, who is devoted to him and will not leave him. During the first act, Valentine is visited in succession by his friends Scandal and Tattle, by Trapland, a scrivener, from whom he has borrowed money, and by Mrs. Frail, the gay and pretty aunt of Angelica. Their dialogue displays, besides the unparalleled wit of each speaker, the despairing conditions to which the fortunes of Valentine are reduced.

The father of Angelica is the ridiculous old astrologer Foresight, in whose house the second act opens. His daughter descends, greets him, teases him, and rides away in her sedan. Sir Sampson Legend, the father of Valentine, presents himself to "old Nostradamus" Foresight, with the intention of informing him that he is about to disinherit Valentine, who will thereupon cease to be an eligible suitor for the hand of Angelica. The two old gentlemen, however, fall into a ludicrous discussion about celestial spheres, sextiles, and fiery trigons on the one side, and the Grand Mogul's slipper, Egyptian mummies, and indiscretions of the court of the King of Bantam on the other, for Sir Sampson has been a great traveller in his day. While they are wrangling, Valentine enters, and he and his father have one of the most admirable scenes in all comedy, where the question of hereditary responsibility is gone into with a seriousness that is unusual on Congreve's cynical stage. The end of it is Sir Sampson will give his son four thousand pounds to pay his debts with, but on condition that he resigns all claim to the estate on behalf of his younger brother Ben, the sailor, who is now returned from a long voyage. Valentine retires, but although he has been so ill received he is satisfied, for he has been seen to treat his father with respect. His visit, however, leaves him as uncertain as ever in what light Angelica regards him.

The stage being now empty, the lively sisters Mrs. Foresight and Mrs. Frail come on to divert us. Mrs. Foresight adopts the most prudish attitude towards Mrs. Frail, and at last accuses her of having an assignation at a place called The World's End. Mrs. Frail denies everything, when Mrs. Foresight, to clinch the accusation, produces an object, and says, "Where did you lose this gold bodkin? Oh sister! sister!" Upon which Mrs. Frail makes the unexpected and wholly delightful return, "Well, if you go to that, where did you find this bodkin? Oh, sister! sister!" They determine that it is worse than useless to spy upon one another, and take a humorous vow of mutual fidelity. Frail then acknowledges that she wants to marry Ben, who now, by Valentine's misfortune, is to inherit the Legend estates. Ben, however, is betrothed to marry Mrs. Foresight's step-daughter Prue. The precious pair determine to make Prue marry Mr. Tattle, and so to leave Ben free for Mrs. Frail. The act closes with a scene full of broad humour, indeed too broad sometimes, between Tattle and Prue, who are purposely left together by the sisters. Prue, though so young and ignorant, proves as adroit a flirt "as if she had been born and bred in Covent Garden."

In the third act, Tattle, flying from Prue, finds Angelica and Valentine together, while Scandal jeers at and banters each in turn. They all unite to torture with their wit the bragging and incautious Tattle. The scene closes with "A nymph and a swain to Apollo once prayed," one of the most graceful and most cynical of Congreve's lyrics. But Sir Sampson rushes in with a roar; he has heard that his son Ben, the sea-dog, has arrived. At this Valentine slips away, "we are the twin-stars," he says, "and cannot shine in one sphere." As he goes, he makes an appeal to Angelica, but she declares she cannot come to any resolution. She turns, when he is gone, to Sir Sampson in a pique, and declares roundly that she wishes nothing but estates in a husband, and that no one would now induce her to marry Valentine, a sentiment that Sir Sampson is vigorously applauding, when Ben rolls in. He talks in a big voice, and with such a rough volley of tarpaulin slang, that Angelica, the superfine, swears ironically that "Mr. Benjamin is the veriest wag in nature, an absolute sea-wit." She is soon appeased, however, and Ben is left alone with Prue, his little betrothed.

The next scene is comedy holding both its sides; the ill-matched couple quarrel till she calls him "stinking tar-barrel," and he says that she is worse than "a Lapland witch." Frail and Foresight, who have been listening, enter, and while Foresight hurries Prue away, Frail stays behind to console the outraged Ben. Sir Sampson and Foresight come by, chuckling; there shall be a wedding to-morrow, and Ben must marry Prue. Their mirth is checked by Slander, who enters with a long face, and has bad news to break to them. Valentine's mind has given way under the strain of his emotions, and he is raving mad. Sir Sampson at once declares that he believes it to be a pretence to avoid signing the conveyance, but he will come with a lawyer and force the rogue to sign. The act prolongs itself with unnecessary pleasantries, but closes at last with Ben's promise to throw off Prue and marry Mrs. Frail. Ben says good-night to the ladies, and sings "A soldier and a sailor" to them before he goes off to the tavern for a can of beer.

The fourth act opens next morning at Valentine's lodgings. The mock-patient is prepared by Scandal and Jeremy to receive the most compromising visitors. Angelica is the first to arrive, and is not successful in her attempt to conceal her anxiety; Scandal pretends to think her visit is tyrannically made "to insult her ruined lover, and make manifest the cruel triumphs of her beauty," and she is being moved almost to tears, when she sees Scandal wink to Jeremy, and suspects a trick at once. She rounds upon them, having recovered her *savoir-faire*, and declaring it to be unnecessary for her to see the poor demented fellow, she and her maid take their leave. Next arrive Sir Sampson and Buckram the conveyancer. They have to be introduced, and so, after a while, the scene opens, and Valentine is discovered, lying in a state of disorder on his couch. Sir Sampson is convinced that it is a genuine case of insanity; Valentine rolls off a series of wonderful apostrophes, and rates the lawyer till he flies off in a panic, declaring Valentine *non compos*, and quite unfit to sign any deed. Valentine promptly recovers as soon as Buckram is gone, sighs, and sinks on his knee to gain his father's blessing. Sir Sampson makes sure of his son's sanity, and then rushes out to fetch Buckram back once more; but the lawyer's return brings Valentine's fit on again, and more violently than ever. Sir Sampson has to explain to Ben that the estate cannot come to him at present, and hints moreover that he may marry again himself. On hearing this Mrs. Frail's interest in Ben instantly wanes, and, calling him a porpoise, she jilts him. Mrs. Foresight now proposes that her sister should try to engage herself, during his madness, to Valentine. The latter enters into the idea, and pretends to take Frail for Angelica, offering to marry her at dead of night at once, with Endymion and the Moon for witnesses. While he is perplexing everybody, the real Angelica comes again; Valentine at once informs her of his trick, but she pretends to disbelieve him, and persists in treating him as if he was actually mad. This act is adorned with an exceedingly delicate and musical lyric, "I tell thee, Charmion, could I time retrieve."

Sir Sampson, who reminds himself that he is only fifty, begins to think that the best way out of the imbroglio will be for him in person to marry Angelica and her fortune. Angelica, for certain ends, is not unwilling to allow him to indulge this preposterous fancy. Tattle also has designs on Angelica, as Frail has on Valentine, and the next thing we hear is, that under close disguise, each thinking the other was our hero or our heroine, Tattle and Frail have been irrevocably wedded. Valentine appears, and, believing that Angelica is genuinely indifferent to him, expresses his readiness to sign the conveyance, which will double her fortune if she marries Sir Sampson. But Angelica snatches the deed from him, and tears it into fragments, while the fiddlers whom Sir Sampson had ordered for his wedding strike up for the auspicious nuptials of Valentine and Angelica :—

> The miracle to-day is, that we find
> A lover true ; not, that a woman's kind.

There is one excellent point about this plot, namely that, having never represented vice as supremely interesting, it closes with a deliberate concession of good fortune to virtue. With those critics who have found Angelica hard and unsympathetic, I cannot agree. To me she is one of the most delightful of all comic heroines ; refined and distinguished in nature, she refuses to wear her heart upon her sleeve, and her learned young spark, with his airs of the academic beau, has to deserve her, or seem to deserve her, before she yields to his somewhat impudent suit. If she tricks him it is only when she finds him tricking her, and the artifice in neither case is very serious. No, Angelica is charming in her presence of mind and lady-like dignity, and reigns easily first among the creations, not only of Congreve, but of post-Restoration comedy down to Goldsmith. She is the comic sister of Belvidera, and these two preserve that corrupt and cynical stage from moral contumely.

One minor character in *Love for Love* deserves special attention. Ben Legend, the "absolute sea-wit," is the founder of a long line of stage-sailors, of whom he is the earliest specimen. Mr. Hannay, with the natural desire of a biographer to give the glory to Smollett, has depreciated Congreve's creation, and says that Ben is "a landsman's sailor, drawn by a man who was not familiar enough with more than the outside of the life to give vitality to the picture." On this point a critic, who is also a landsman, may hesitate to express his opinion; but lack of vitality hardly strikes one as characteristic of Ben. The tarpaulin type seems faithfully studied and vigorously drawn, and I doubt much whether Congreve could have created so salt a sailor, with a smack of the very sea about him, out of his internal consciousness. The moment Ben is slightly thwarted he remembers he has another voyage to make. We sailors, he says, are merry folk; we come home once a year, get rid of a little money, and then put off with the next fair wind. Mrs. Frail gets the blind side of him by the bold use of a marine metaphor, and he wishes he had Prue at sea to give her a salt eel for her supper. When his family sentimentalizes over his desperate voyages, he has no other reply than, "Been far enough, an that be all!" Good or bad, no sailor in fiction—except, as Mr. Hannay acutely points out, those in *The Fair Quaker of Kent*—approached him till the days of Jack Rattlin and Tom Bowling.

The book of *Love for Love* (published May 9, 1695 [1]), was dedicated to Lord Dorset in a short preface, where the author confesses the main error of his play, its prolixity, and tells us that one scene, probably that between Scandal and Foresight in the middle of the third act, had to be omitted in representation. *Love for Love* is by far the longest of Congreve's five plays, and although no reader can ever have wished it shorter, it must have taken a very long time in representation, especially as it contains

[1] "London Gazette."

no less than three songs for music and a dance. The play was very successful in book form, and several editions of 1695 exist. It had an unprecedented run, for, with certain breaks, it continued to be played at Lincoln's Inn Fields for the remainder of the year. The only one fresh play brought out that season at the new theatre seems to have been the *Pyrrhus*, of Charles Hopkins, the first tragedy of a young poet who had gained the warm friendship of Dryden, and who might have won a considerable reputation if he had lived. To *Pyrrhus* Congreve contributed a prologue, which was published with the play. This is a witty piece of occasion, comparing the serried ranks of the two theatres to the armies of Rome and of Epirus.

One of Congreve's most agreeable characteristics was his friendliness. We have no record of his falling out with any one, and he had the art to remain on intimate terms with those who could not speak to one another. With Dryden and with Swift, with Dennis and with Pope, with Addison and with Steele, no matter what anger ruled in their celestial minds, nor what dissensions arrived, Congreve was always on the friendliest footing. Of the men whose names have just been cited, John Dennis, the Sir Tremendous of Pope's satire, was unquestionably the most choleric, but at all times Dennis was on terms of unbroken civility with Congreve. In consequence of this acquaintance, and of some vanity no doubt on Dennis' part as the public friend of so eminent a poet, we get in the latter part of 1695 some glimpse of Congreve's private life. In 1696 (December 12, 1695 [1])

[1] "London Gazette."

Dennis published a little volume of *Letters upon several Occasions*, a tolerably rich mine of little facts to the literary historian of the age. This book consisted of letters written to Dennis by Dryden, Wycherley, Congreve, and Walter Moyle, with the replies of Dennis.

At this time Dennis was about forty years of age. His characteristic violence of temper, ending in his stabbing a fellow-commoner of Caius, had cut short his promising academic life at Cambridge. After long wandering over the face of Europe, he had made his entry into London life about the same time as Congreve himself, though at an age much more advanced. He had some wealth, lavish extravagance, and a restless ambition; he published copies of verses, satires, criticisms, and had ready for performance one comedy at least. The volume of which we are speaking shows that he claimed the acquaintance of the first wits of the age, and that his claim was not rejected. He dedicates his book to Charles Montague, with a promise that that great man shall nowhere in it find himself outside the circle of his distinguished acquaintance. The first letter in the book is addressed from his Cornwall house, by Walter Moyle, to Congreve, and seems to give an account of a lost poem by the latter:—

> A humorous description of John Abassus, a nickname given to a stupid Sussex squire, fond of plays and poems, who came up to town, as he said, "to see the Poets of the Age," and was by some of them introduced among the wits of Will's Coffee-house in Covent Garden, among whom they admitted him, under the form of a poetical consecration, as a member of their society.

This *Consecration of John Abassus* seems to have been

thrown away, as beneath the dignity of the Muse. To regain it we would sacrifice all Congreve's solemn pastorals and perfunctory pindarics. We gather from Moyle's letter, which is dated October 7, 1695, that Wycherley at this time took the chair at Will's Coffee-house, when he was in town. It also begs Congreve to tell Moyle what progress he has made with his tragedy, which shows that *The Mourning Bride* was already partly written. The letters were all of recent date when Dennis printed them. The earliest communication from Congreve is an essay on Humour in Comedy, sent to Dennis on the 10th of July, 1695. This essay treats a subject so interesting on the lips of our greatest comic dramatist, that we may examine it somewhat minutely.

Congreve begins by confessing that, in his opinion, the English have not excelled in humour by any means so universally as is usually supposed. He conceives that what is often taken for humour should be described as wit; no doubt the dialogue in his own plays, which displays the very quintessence of wit, had often, to his annoyance, been praised for its "humour." He continues:—

> I have observed that when a few things have been wittily and pleasantly spoken by any character in a comedy, it has been very usual for those who make their remarks on a play, while it is acting, to say "Such a thing is very humorously said, there is a great deal of humour in that part." Thus the character of the person speaking, it may be, surprisingly and pleasantly, is mistaken for a character of humour, which indeed is a character of wit.

He deals very severely with the ordinary so-called comedies of the day, having, no doubt, in his mind such follies as those to which Ravenscroft, D'Urfey, and Settle were happy to sign their names, "stuffed," as Congreve puts it, "with grotesque figures and farce-fools." The comedies of Shadwell, even, belonged to this class, nor were Dryden and Southerne quite clean of this pitch of redundant absurdity. Congreve demanded a far higher ideal of comic literature :—

> For my part, I am as willing to laugh as anybody, and as easily diverted with an object truly ridiculous ; but, at the same time, I never care for seeing things that force me to entertain low thoughts of my nature. I don't know how it is with you, but I confess freely to you, I could never look long upon a monkey without very mortifying reflections, though I never heard anything to the contrary why that creature is not originally of a distinct species. As I do not think humour exclusive of wit, neither do I think it inconsistent with folly, but I think the follies should be only such as men's humour may incline them to, and not follies entirely abstracted from both humour and nature.

It is perhaps not too wild a guess to conjecture that in this sarcastic description Congreve was pointing at *The Canterbury Guests*, a miserable comedy by Ravenscroft, which the Patentees of the Theatre Royal had just brought out. With great critical acumen, he goes on to distinguish certain classes of characteristics which are commonly, and incorrectly, presented as matter of humour. Personal defects, although Ben Jonson has made use of them in *The Fox*, are not to be properly introduced into comedy, nor external habit of body, nor, without careful discrimination, even affectation, because humour is a natural growth, and affectation the result of industry. Congreve then passes to a particular and very interesting review of humour as displayed in the great comedies of Jonson, and presently, not without an expression of diffidence, he advances a definition of humour, which he takes to be "a singular and unavoidable manner of doing or saying anything, peculiar and natural to one man only, by which his speech and actions are distinguished from those of other men." He is inclined to deny it to women, or states, at least, that, so far as his experience goes, "if ever anything does appear comical or ridiculous in a woman, I think it is little more than an acquired folly." He then proceeds to remark that the diversity of humour, to be noted in the human race, might seem to afford endless matter for the writing of comedies. Yet it is not so, and only a very small selection of whimsical natures really lend themselves to dramatic development. He closes with a defence of English eccentricity, which is as true as it was two hundred years ago:—

There is more of humour in our English comic writers than in any other. I do not at all wonder at it, for I look upon humour to be almost of English growth; at least, it does not seem to have found such increase on any other soil. And what appears to me to be the reason of it is the great freedom, privilege, and liberty which the common people of England enjoy. Any man that has a humour is under no restraint or fear of giving it vent; they have a proverb among them which, may be, will show the bent and genius of the people as well as a longer discourse, "He that will have a May-pole, shall have a Maypole." This is a maxim with them, and their practice is agreeable to it. I believe something considerable too may be ascribed to their feeding so much on flesh, and the grossness of their diet in general. But let the physicians agree about that.

On the 30th of May, 1695, Narcissus Luttrel notes

that "Mr. Charnock Heron, Mr. Clark and Mr. Congreve, the poet, are made commissioners of the hackney-coaches in the place of Mr. Ashurst, Mr. Overbury and Mr. Isham, who resigned." The cause of the resignation was that the salary of the office had been suddenly cut down from £200 a year to £100. For some time this small post under Government appears to have been the only such emolument given to the poet. Congreve reminds us of the legendary Civil Servant who asked for a week's holiday on the day he received his appointment, in order to get used to the office, since he immediately proceeded to Tunbridge Wells to drink steel for an attack of the spleen. Though still in his twenty-sixth year, he seems to have already sapped his constitution. After both Moyle and Dennis have upbraided him for his silence, at last, on the 11th of August, he writes to them from the Wells. He is not so fond of the country, but that he would rather read a description of a landscape in town than see the real thing. A passage from this letter is worth quoting :—

I wish for you very often, that I might recommend you to some new acquaintance that I have made here, and think very well worth the keeping, I mean idleness and a good stomach. You would not think how people eat here, everybody has the appetite of an ostrich, and as they drink steel in the morning, so I believe at noon they could digest iron. But sure you will laugh at me for calling idleness a new acquaintance, when, to your knowledge, the greater part of my business is no better. Ay, but hear the comfort of the change; I am idle now, without taking pains to be so, or to make other people so, for poetry is neither in my head nor in my heart. I know not whether these waters may have any communication with Lethe, but sure I am they have none with the streams of Helicon. I have often wondered how those wicked writers of lampoons could crowd together such quantities of execrable verses, tagged with bad rhymes, as I have formerly seen sent from this place, but I am half of opinion now, that this well is an anti-Hippocrene. What if we should get a quantity of the water privately conveyed into the cistern at Will's Coffee-house for an experiment?

He proceeds to say that he thinks something very comical and novel might be put together for the stage by studying the oddities of such a place as Tunbridge Wells. It is a great pity that Congreve's growing indolence forbad that he himself should do it. It would have been nothing to his disadvantage that Shadwell, nearly a quarter of a century earlier, had sketched a similar lively scene, in his own way, in his *Epsom Wells*. The Tunbridge Spa had itself been made the subject of an anonymous comedy, in 1678; this I have never come across, but by 1695, whatever may have been its success for the moment, it was, of course, forgotten.

During the autumn and winter of 1695 Congreve was slowly writing and polishing the scenes of his tragedy, *The Mourning Bride*, but he also found time for several small occasional writings. His *Ode to the King*, printed in folio with the date 1695 on the title-page, was published, according to the "London Gazette," on the 17th of October. This ode is one of the strongest proofs we possess of the limited nature of Congreve's genius, and of his own ignorance of its limitations. It is an extremely lengthy example of that horrid kind of bastard Pindarics which had been introduced, for the chastisement of English literature, about forty years before, by Cowley. It was Congreve who, later on, was destined to purify English ode, and return it to its classic form; we may therefore suppose, if we like, that he wished to make a helot of himself by producing, first of all, the worst specimen of the false ode on record. This Pindaric on the Taking of Namur opens by the startled poet asking his Muse why his pinions have suddenly spread, and why his oaten pipe has turned into a lyre. Like the mother of Sisera, he replies to his own query:—

> William alone my feeble voice can raise,
> * * * * *
> For by his name my verse shall be preferred,
> Borne like a lark upon an eagle's wing.

The attempt to describe the campaign and its battles in detestable groups of noisy alexandrines is simply disastrous, and it would be criminal to linger any longer within the precincts of a poem that does not possess one tolerable line.

Congreve was more appropriately occupied just before Christmas. Southerne had chosen to remain with the Patentees of the Theatre Royal, and when he brought out his *Oroonoko*, a romantic tragedy of very high sentimental merit, Dryden contributed a prologue, and Congreve, very gracefully, concealing the rival in the friend, an epilogue. These poems duly adorned the printed book of the play, published on the 12th of December, 1695. Congreve's lines were spoken by Mrs. Verbruggen. In July, 1696, when Dryden brought out the only play of his son John, the MS. of which had been sent to him from Italy, the *Husband his own Cuckold*, Congreve paid it the same compliment. The opening lines of this prologue are curious, and cannot very easily be accounted for:

> This year has been remarkable two ways,
> For blooming poets and for blasted plays;
> We've been by much appearing plenty mocked,
> At once both tantalized and overstocked.
> Our authors, too, by their success of late,
> Begin to think third days are out of date;
> What can the cause be that our plays won't keep,
> Unless they have a rot, some years, like sheep?
> For our parts we confess we're quite ashamed
> To read such weekly bills of poets damned.

It is true that 1696 was the year when a whole nest of dramatic singing-birds first took flight. Gould, Lord Landsdowne, Colley Cibber, and the three new Muses, Mrs. Pix, Mrs. Manley, and Mrs. Trotter, all made their *début* that year; but it is not recorded that all or most of these new plays were failures. During the remainder of this year Congreve is perfectly invisible to us. Perhaps he was entirely absorbed by his duties at the Hackney Coach Licenses Office.

The tragedy which had been so long preparing was concluded at last. Nothing seems to be more capricious than the amount of time required by a playwright for the construction of his pieces. Victor Hugo seldom took more than three weeks to write a five-act tragedy; Congreve was for not less than three years mainly occupied with the same amount and character of work. It has usually been supposed that *The Mourning Bride* was brought out at Lincoln's Inn Fields late in 1697. This may now be considered as disproved by an entry in the "London Gazette," which shows that the first edition of the play in quarto appeared on the 11th of March of that year. It was customary to print plays about a fortnight after they were put on the stage, and we shall therefore, in all probability, be safe in attributing the first performance of Congreve's tragedy to the close of February. The poet's friends welcomed *The Mourning Bride* with no small anxiety. Congreve's splendid success in Comedy offered no safeguard of his ability to please in this more solemn kind of writing. It was, however, carefully put on the stage. Betterton, the immortal youth, although now between sixty and seventy, returned to one of those parts in which he had gained his greatest triumphs, the ranting hero-characters that Lee had written for him twenty years before. Osmyn was safe in his hands; Verbruggen, now much ripened and improved by experience, was excellently fitted for the King; while of the female parts, it could but be confessed that the melancholy passion of Almeria and the wayward majesty of Zara were created for the Bracegirdle and the Barry. Everything went as favourably as possible. Congreve never enjoyed, with either of his comedies, so complete and lasting a success, and *The Mourning Bride* continued to be a stock piece for nearly a century.

It has been the habit to quote *The Mourning Bride* as the very type of bad declamatory tragedy. No doubt Dr. Johnson did it harm by that extravagant eulogy in which he selected one fragment as unsurpassed in the poetry of all time. But if we compare it, not with those tragedies of the age of Elizabeth, studded with occasional naïve felicities, which it is just now the fashion to admire with some extravagance, but with what England and even France produced from 1650 to the revival of romantic taste, *The Mourning Bride* will probably take a place close after what is best in Otway and Racine. It will bear comparison, as I would venture to assert, with Southerne's *Fatal Marriage* or with Crébillon's *Rhadamiste et Zénobie*, and will not be pronounced inferior to these excellent and famous tragedies in dramatic interest, or genuine grandeur of sentiment, or beauty of language. It has done what no other of these special rivals has done, outside the theatre of Racine, it has contributed to the everyday fashion of its country several well-worn lines. But it is not every one who says that "Music has charms to soothe a savage breast" or that "Hell knows no fury like a woman scorn'd," who would be able to tell where the familiar sentiment first occurs.

From what source Congreve borrowed the plot of *The Mourning Bride* does not appear to be known; perhaps he invented it himself. It is clear and fairly interesting, but improbable. The scene is laid at Granada at some remote period of the Middle Ages. When the action opens, Almeria, the heroine, is discovered alone, in mourning robes, listening to dying music. She laments the decease, on the preceding day, of the captive King of Valencia, long kept barbarously incarcerated by her own cruel father, Manuel, King of Granada. During a previous revolution of the body politic, while Granada was down and Valencia up, Almeria was secretly married, on board ship, to Alphonso, Prince of Valencia, but he was drowned the same day. Her father who knows nothing of this incident, desires her to marry Garcia, his brave general, the son of a certain meddlesome Polonius named

Gonsalez, who is the prime minister of Granada. When the curtain rises the king is momentarily expected back from a victorious campaign; he enters, and is annoyed to find Almeria in black. There is a remarkably subtle and dramatic speech in which it gradually dawns upon him that his daughter is in mourning because she secretly regrets his conquest of Valencia. He bids her hasten to receive Garcia as her bridegroom, and as she leaves, the prisoners of the recent war are brought on the stage. Among them is a haughty beauty, Zara, of whom the king is already enamoured, and a very handsome youth of military aspect, named Osmyn, in whom Zara appears to take a more than friendly interest. The personages of the tragedy are now all before us, and the rest of the action is occupied with the intrigue of their adventures.

The second act is the best in the play, and the *mise-en-scène* suggested in it is so mysterious and beautiful that one wishes that a modern management might be at the pains to produce it. The scene is the aisle of a vast cathedral, through which, at the back, is perceived the royal mausoleum. Osmyn has been seen to disappear among the tombs, and accordingly Garcia, with Heli and Perez, friends of Osmyn, pursue him, but, after some important comments, fail to discover him, and retire. Almeria and her maid then come forward, and, as she enters the cathedral, Almeria utters those splendid lines to which Dr. Johnson awarded his partly just, but certainly excessive, praise. It may be convenient to quote the passage which Dr. Johnson selected as "the most poetical paragraph in the whole mass of English poetry":—

Almeria. It is a fancied noise, for all is hush'd.
Leonora. It bore the accent of a human voice.
Alm. It was thy fear, or else some transient wind
Whistling thro' hollows of this vaulted aisle.
We'll listen !
Leon. Hark !
Alm. No ! all is hush'd, and still as death ! 'Tis dreadful !
How reverend is the face of this tall pile,
Whose ancient pillars rear their marble heads
To bear aloft its arched and ponderous roof,
By its own weight made stedfast and immoveable,
Looking tranquillity ! It strikes an awe
And terror on my aching sight ; the tombs
And monumental caves of death look cold,
And shoot a chillness to my trembling heart.
Give me thy hand !
Oh speak to me ! nay, speak ! and let me hear
Thy voice ! My own affrights me with its echoes.

Almeria is proceeding to visit, in the mausoleum, the body of the King of Valencia, father to her lost husband of a day. Her sorrows overwhelm her, and in an ecstasy of grief she calls on Alphonso ; when, suddenly, from the tomb itself, Alphonso rises. The seeming miracle nearly destroys her ; but it is easily explained. Alphonso, who had not been drowned after all, in order to approach her in the enemy's country, has been captured under the title of Osmyn. All might now be well but for the unfortunate passion of Zara, who has fallen in love with him as Osmyn, not dreaming of his real title and condition. As, so long ago, in the Sicily of Moschus, Pan loved Echo, and Echo a satyr, and that satyr only Lyde, so while the king loves Zara, Zara only looks at Osmyn, and Osmyn is Alphonso secretly wedded to Almeria. It is easy to realize the sort of complications which ensue out of such a scheme of intrigue as this.

The last act is rather bloody, and too much involved in the sound and fury of Nat Lee. Osmyn has for some time past been in prison, his life hanging on the caprice of Zara, who now fondles and now threatens to destroy him. The Valencians have raised an army, and clamour for their prince, but the King of Granada, a very weak creature, cannot make up his mind to set him free. At last he determines to have him murdered in prison, and, to spite his daughter, he orders the robes of Osmyn to be taken from him, and while the Valencian prince is executed somewhere else, the king will lie in the cell of Osmyn, in the dusk, robed like him, and will challenge the truth from the terror of Almeria. This is dreadfully improbable, as an incident, but it leads to some very showy "business." For Gonsalez, discovering a plot for the release of Osmyn-Alphonso, steals into the cell, and, thinking all will be safe if once the prisoner is murdered, stabs the disguised king to the heart, and steals out again, conceiving Alphonso to be his victim. Zara follows, meaning to release Alphonso, finds him dead, as she supposes, and quaffs cold poison; while Almeria, rushing in after her, and being under the same impression, is only just saved from doing the like by the arrival of the real Alphonso, who has entered Granada as a conqueror. It would be rather a fine ending if the body of the king did not continue to spout and gush with gore in scene after scene. But there is too much blood by half in the body of this old man, and the consequences are quite disgusting. It is, however, to be noted as somewhat consoling, that at the close of the piece the hero and heroine are still alive, and not gulphed in an indiscriminate slaughter.

The blank verse of *The Mourning Bride* deserves some consideration, because it seems to be the model on which most eighteenth-century unrhymed iambics were formed. It is the parent of Thomson's, as that is of Cowper's and of Wordsworth's blank verse. When the heroic tragedies went out of fashion, and dramatic blank verse was reverted to by Dryden and Otway, those writers took the easy versification of Shakespeare's later time, with the incessant extra syllable, as their model. Lee, who was influenced by Milton, is much more sparing of this redundancy, and Congreve follows Lee rather than any other dramatist. His real model is, however, Milton, and it is curious to trace in his tragic blank verse a respectful study of that impeccable master. There are few inversions of rhythm; the break or cæsura is very well managed, and when a variation of stress is admitted, it can almost always be justified in *Paradise Lost.* For instance—

> "My fáther's voíce ! hóllow it sóunds, and cálls,"

with its inversion of the third stress, reminds us of Milton's

> "For óne restráint, lórds of the wórld besides ;"

and Congreve's

> "Crúel, crúel, o móre than kílling óbject"

is paralleled in *Paradise Lost* by

> "Úniversal reproách, far wórse to beár."

The double inversion of stress, too, in Congreve's beautiful line—

> "Wás it the dóleful béll tólling for Déath?"

could no doubt be justified by Miltonic practice, though I doubt whether in one single instance of a triple inversion Congreve does not pass outside the record of any existing specimen of *Paradise Lost.* The line is—

> "Óf a fáther's fóndness those íll aróse."

These exceptions are worth noting, because they are introduced by a poet—who thoroughly understood what he was doing—into a system of blank verse more conservative than any which had been seen since the beginning of the seventeenth century. The direct influence of the verse of *The Mourning Bride* may be detected in the tragedies of Young, and then in his *Night Thoughts.*

The Mourning Bride enjoyed a greater pecuniary success than any other play of Congreve's. It ran, at first, for at least thirteen nights, but this was a small part of its importance; it took the place which Lee's *Rival Ladies* had taken as the fashionable tragedy of its age. Through the next generation, when Rowe laid siege to the town with one lachrymose and sentimental tragedy after another, Rowe, with all his skill, could never oust *The Mourning Bride*, or write what the ladies would, after a few nights, determine to prefer to it. It is not to be questioned that this play continued to be a more constant source of income to Congreve than any one of his comedies.

On the 4th of May, 1697, according to Luttrel, a small increase was made to Congreve's official income, as, in addition to his hackney-coaches, he was made a "commissioner for hawkers and pedlars." On the 5th of October, Dr. Woodward wrote to Evelyn, "Mr. Congreve is, I hear, engaged in a poem on occasion of the Peace, and all who are acquainted with the performance of this gentleman expect something very extraordinary." Accordingly, on the 18th of November,[1] on occasion of His Majesty's landing, was published a folio pamphlet entitled *The Birth of the Muse*, dedicated to Montague. This is the longest of Congreve's miscellaneous poems, and is written carefully in the heroic couplet, but with tiresome and "needless" introduction of alexandrines. It consists of a vision of the conduct of the universe, rapidly passing through the creation of Britannia and the reign of Eliza, to the glories and triumphs of William III. It is a very poor affair, and contains nothing prettier than the lines describing England under Elizabeth—

> Above the waves she lifts her silver head,
> And looks a Venus born from Ocean's bed ;
> For rolling years her happy fortunes smile,
> And fates propitious bless the beauteous isle ;
> To worlds remote she wide extends her reign.
> And wields the trident of the stormy main ;
> Thus on the base of empire firm she stands,
> While bright Eliza rules the willing lands.

At the close of the poem the author becomes rather

[1] "London Gazette."

blasphemous, but without any intention to offend. Dennis came forward with a performance on the same occasion, and both he and Congreve were immediately ridiculed in an anonymous pamphlet of hudibrastics, entitled *The Justice of Peace.*

CHAPTER III.

WE have now reached the point at which the serene and hitherto scarcely ruffled surface of Congreve's literary life was broken up by a storm of prolonged severity. It is the only crisis which we meet with in his career, but it was epoch-making not for him only, but for dramatic literature in England, and from the evil results of it the popularity of Congreve and even of comedy suffers to the present day. Until now, in describing the poet's successive triumphs on the stage, it has seemed well to refrain from one criticism which must be ever present with the reader of Restoration and Orange comedy, namely, that the language is coarse and the sentiment cynical to an exceedingly reprehensible degree. The fault scarcely lay with the poets of the latest generation. They simply followed a tradition which had existed before they were born. It was when Congreve was an infant that the dramatists had thrown off all shame in language and intention, and that Rochester had summed up the philosophy of anti-puritanical reaction in the audacious couplet :—

> Our sphere of action is life's happiness,
> And he who thinks beyond, thinks like an ass.

The Puritans, unhappily for our civilization, had condemned the innocent with the guilty pleasures of life, and had included poetry, painting, and music among the deadly sins. The Royalists, in returning to power, had taken these enjoyments into favour, together with those others which more legitimately fell under the lash of religious ardour. Out of all this there grew an obliquity of moral vision, a mixing of patriotism and debauchery, gaming, drinking, and the Church of England, loyalty, dice and church-attendance, in an incongruous *olla podrida* of things not unbecoming in one of the king's gentlemen.

The fault lay not wholly with the beaux and the orange-girls. The Church, also, was indulgent.[1] Dr. Payne, in his funeral sermon on Queen Mary, praises her Majesty for her love of play-going, card-playing, and other gentle amusements. When we recollect what comedies the Queen is known to have seen and commended, the elegiacial reflection of the divine seems a little startling.

The beaux desired to keep well with the Establishment; they went assiduously to church, and Shadwell describes them, "troops of 'em, posted up in galleries, setting their cravats." They were in the habit, after a hard gallop through life, of making salutory ends,

[1] The editor of the grave and pious Sir Richard Baker's posthumous *Theatrum Triumphans*, a fierce attack on Prynne, speaks of the objection of the Puritans to plays as being worthy of Bedlam, and congratulates English people on now (in 1670) being "so happy as to be allowed the use of their own eyes and reason again."

and even John Wilmot, Lord Rochester, the little Nero of British verse, lies decently embalmed in Burnet's decorous memoir. "His knowledge and observation qualified him to have been one of the most extraordinary men, not only of his nation, but of the age he lived in, and I do verily believe that if God had thought fit to have continued him longer in the world, he had been the wonder and delight of all that knew him," says the future Bishop of Salisbury, who has just before been giving us a report of how difficult it was for the noble earl, on his death-bed, to understand that a man should be "curbed to such a narrowness," as to put any restraint upon his natural appetites. The real excuse for the churchmen is that they probably did not know exactly what was said and done in the theatre. The king applauded; the place of the Church was to bow. The clergy did not visit the theatre, and were not too careful to analyse the royal amusements.

We might expect that after nearly thirty years of increasing looseness of manners, a crisis in history would bring with it a clearer atmosphere. But it remains a fact that the Revolution of 1688 was not favourable to morals, and the plays that directly succeeded the accession of William III. were astounding in their looseness of tongue and gait.[1] The drama had steadily grown more incongruous, and the need to spice plays with

[1] In his ingenious and learned book on the England of the eighteenth century, M. Alexandre Beljame has collected quite a little anthology of horrors, a posy of poisonous flowers, selected from all the leading writers of this age. It is calculated rather to surprise a decent person.

what would be agreeable to the small and very captious class by which the theatre was supported, tempted each author of a fresh work to risk a still stronger situation, to adopt a still more brazen diction, than his predecessor. Even Voltaire, in the next generation, looking back upon English drama, was shocked at its license, and it is only just to add that it seemed to Voltaire that Congreve had striven to introduce a greater moderation and decency of speech. At all events, let those who would throw a stone at him glance, with averted countenances, at the comedies of Otway and Southerne. They will, at least, absolve Congreve from having attempted to outshame his predecessors. He is never so coarse, he is never so abnormal, as Vanbrugh, his contemporary and successor, often was. He is not one of the worst offenders, and it is probable that he genuinely supposed that he was hardly an offender at all. Such, however, was not the opinion of moralists, and his comedies, by reason of their superlative literary merit, and their superior vitality, have come to be regarded as the very ideal of those plays which ladies were afraid to attend barefaced, and therefore flocked into the pit, side-boxes, and gallery, to listen to in masks which could, at a moment's notice, hide their blushes and preserve for themselves a decent anonymity.

The extraordinary thing was that this license had gone on for nearly forty years without producing a single protest of a serious nature. The Dissenters denounced stage-plays, indeed, but without discrimination; to them Milton's *Comus* and some shameful farce of Ravenscroft displayed no moral distinction. They neither read nor witnessed what they attacked, and no one heeded what they said outside their own communities. But towards the close of 1697 there came some mutterings of moral thunder in higher places. In the preface to his epic of *King Arthur* (not to be confounded with his *Prince Arthur*) Blackmore gently protested against what was obscene and profane in recent poetry, and warned the writers that a future age might come to reject them "with indignation and contempt, as the dishonour of the Muses and the underminers of the public good." Blackmore goes on to praise *The Mourning Bride* in almost unmeasured terms, and it is curious to find Congreve, who was about to be pilloried so savagely, brought forward as a model of chastity for other writers to imitate.

> This tragedy (Blackmore continues) has mightily obtained, and that without the unnatural and foolish mixture of farce and buffoonery, without so much as song or dance to make it more agreeable. By this it appears, that as a sufficient genius can recommend itself, and furnish out abundant matter of pleasure and admiration without the paltry helps above-named, so likewise that the taste of the nation is not so far depraved but that a regular and chaste play will not only be forgiven, but highly applauded. And now there is some reason to hope that our poets will follow this excellent example, and that hereafter no slovenly writer will be so hardy as to offer to our public audiences his obscene and profane pollutions [an allusion, probably, to Vanbrugh's *Provok'd Wife*, published May 31, 1697 [1]], to the great offence of all persons of virtue and good sense. . . . All men must now conclude that 'tis for want of wit and judgment to support them that our poets for the stage apply themselves to such low and unworthy ways to recommend their writings.

[1] "London Gazette."

Blackmore carried, at that moment, some little weight with the literary public, and a month or two later, early in 1698, a sensation was caused, among the vulgar, by the publication of a violent diatribe against the amusements and vices of the age, the *Immorality, Debauchery, and Profaneness* of G. Merriton. Neither the one attack nor the other had any positive importance, but each served to do something to prepare the national conscience for that tremendous blast which Jeremy Collier blew in March, 1698. Every one is familiar with Macaulay's eloquent description of the perfervid character and political isolation of this remarkable man, who had been born near Cambridge in 1650, had early entered the Church, and was now identified with what in these days we should call the extreme High party. He remained staunch to the Jacobites after 1688, and poured forth pamphlet after pamphlet of appeal against the new authority. So lately as 1696 he had been outlawed, in consequence of his absolution of Friend and Parkins on the scaffold, and this outlawry had been solemnly approved of by a committee of the archbishops and ten of the bishops. It was at such a moment, with the leaders of both parties vehemently excited against him, that this intrepid clergyman took up his extremely active pen in defence of literary decency.

Collier's famous volume is not a very common book, and strange to say, in spite of Macaulay's commendation, in this age of reprints, it has never been published since the early part of the eighteenth century. The title is *A Short View of the Immorality and Profaneness of the English Stage, together with the Sense of*

Antiquity upon this Argument. The reader who expects to find Collier's book a piece of ranting pharisaism, or full of the cant of a literary Tartuffe, will be disappointed. The treatment of the subject is severe, but reasonable; the tone is that of a man of the world. Collier—who afterwards, it is only fair to admit, lost his temper and wrote like a fanatic—remains, in the *Short View*, temperate and even gay. He has no objection to poetry in general, or even, theoretically, to drama. He is not engaged in battering the play-house, like Tertullian, or Prynne, or William Law long afterwards. He thinks it a source of frightful iniquity, it is true, not inherently, but in consequence of the licentious practice of existing poets. He lays down, on the contrary, a rule of conduct for the drama; "The business of plays," he tells us, "is to recommend virtue and discountenance vice, to show the uncertainty of human greatness, the sudden turns of fate, and the unhappy conclusions of violence and injustice." This would shelter Shakespeare, Molière, and Calderon from attack, if it went no further; but it wrung the withers of the poets of Collier's day upon the opening page. Yet even here, he was not violent with the heedless rage of a Puritan; he spares a compliment for Congreve, an expression of respect for Dryden. Even of Wycherley he says, "Some people . . . are offensive like beggars for want of necessaries, but this is none of the Plain Dealer's case; he can afford his Muse a better dress when he pleases." The critic even goes out of his way to commend a play which is rather a hard morsel for nineteenth-century prudery to swallow; "Fletcher's *Faithful Shepherdess*," he says, "is remarkably moral, and a sort of exhortation to chastity." After this, it cannot be said that Collier started by being fanatically strait-laced. He became so later on, when the poets had teased and baited him, but in the *Short View* he speaks with remarkable moderation and with a desire to be just. If Congreve and Vanbrugh had met him half-way, it seems possible that they might have turned their most formidable enemy into a friend.

Macaulay has, I think, a little exaggerated the wit of Collier; it is too much to say that "all the modes of ridicule, from broad fun to polished and antithetical sarcasm, were at Collier's command." But Macaulay is no more than just to what is certainly the brightest prose pamphlet of its time, when he records his impression of its vivacity, variety, and glow. In his first section, "The Immodesty of the Stage," Collier hardly ever goes wrong, or makes a random stroke, although, of course, from the nature of the theme, and the squeamishness of the modern reader, it is somewhat difficult to follow him here with any minuteness. He specially attacks the dialogue of Dryden, Congreve, and Vanbrugh, giving quotations enough and to spare to show how reckless they were in depicting to the life scenes of extreme turpitude. He compares the purity of the French drama of Corneille, of the Greek drama of Sophocles, and of the Latin drama of Terence, with the impurity of these ribald English playwrights, and he sums up his whole argument against the immodesty of the contemporary stage in these words:—

By what has been offered, it appears that the present English stage is superlatively scandalous. It exceeds the liberties of all times and countries. It has not so much as the poor plea of a precedent, to which most other ill things may claim a pretence. 'Tis mostly mere discovery and invention, a new world of vice found out, and planted with all the industry imaginable. Aristophanes himself, how bad soever in other respects, does not amplify, and flourish, and run through all the topics of lewdness, like these men. The *Miscellany Poems* are likewise horribly licentious. They are sometimes collections from antiquity, and often the worst parts of the worst poets. And, to mend the matter, the Christian translation is more nauseous than the pagan original. Such stuff, I believe, was never seen and suffered before. In a word, if poverty and disease, the dishonour of families, and the debauchery of kingdoms, are such valuable advantages, then I confess these books deserve encouragement.

The second section of the *Short View* deals with "The Profaneness of the Stage." Collier divides his indictment of this class of disorders into two parts: first, cursing and swearing; and, second, abuse of religion and Holy Scripture. In what he says under the former head he is very amusing. He notes that heroes swear on the stage, and so do poltroons; gentlemen are profane, and so are clowns. Oaths form the universal garniture of dialogue, and a very pretty ornament to conversation. Love and battle, success and disappointment, are alike occasions for swearing. Where an expression is flat, an oath will make it musical and round. Some of the poets, indeed, use profanity as their magazine of rhetoric and of reason. Congreve is shown to be a sad offender, and Vanbrugh "particularly rampant and scandalous," while Shakespeare and Ben Jonson are commended for their sobriety in this regard. After this, it seems an anticlimax to mention that the 3rd of James I., chap. 21, makes profane swearing a penal offence. But Collier regains his good sense and his lucid playful reasonableness in the following very clever argument for the exclusion of oaths from the stage :—

> Swearing in the play-house is an ungentlemanly, as well as an unchristian practice. The ladies make a considerable part of the audience. Now, swearing before women is reckoned a breach of good behaviour, and therefore a civil atheist will forbear it. The custom seems to go upon this presumption, that the impressions of religion are strongest in women, and more generally spread, and that it must be very disagreeable to them to hear the Majesty of God treated with so little respect. Besides, oaths are a boisterous and tempestuous sort of conversation, generally the effects of passion, and spoken with noise and heat. Swearing looks like the beginning of a quarrel, to which women have an aversion, as being neither armed by nature, nor disciplined by custom for such rough disputes. A woman will start at a soldier's oath almost as much as at the report of his pistol, and therefore a well-bred man will no more swear than fight in the company of ladies.

Here Collier is seen at his best. He goes down among his adversaries like a gentlemanly Tory parson, and takes a *pastillio de bocca* out of a beau's box of beaten gold, while he smilingly upbraids him for his incongruities. He is absolutely courageous in attack, always, but as yet he is careful to have his periwig neatly careened, his cravat-string sprucely fastened. The cushion-thumping, the rage of the frowsy Puritan preacher, are for the present as far removed as possible from Collier's tone of fine breeding. This is a point which deserves to be dwelt upon, especially as Leigh Hunt's unfortunate phrases, "half-witted" and "a violent fool," have never been entirely discredited.

Up to the point we have now reached it cannot be held that Collier had said a word too much. But he was about to go wrong. He was too distinctly a parson not to wish to divide his sermon into heads, and he was too lavish in the length of his discourse. He held the unhappy playwrights prisoners while he "argued high, and argued low, and also argued round about him." The second branch of his second head was "Abuse of Religion," and on this subject he mingled a great many things which were absurd with not a few that were true and salutary. Wildblood, in Dryden's *Mock-Astrologer*, swears by Mahomet; a stage-devil, at the close of the same play, sneezes because he has been too long out of the fire; Dorax, in *Don Sebastian*, refuses to trust Heaven with his revenge; Valentine, in *Love for Love*, raving in his assumed madness, cries "I am Truth!" These are examples of four different kinds of supposed stage-profanity, the citation of which did Collier's cause little real service.

Let us consider these typical cases. That Collier should object to the name of false Mahound being taken in vain, seems to show some want of estimation of the real meaning of an oath. It is at all events difficult to wrest this into a profane expression; it is as innocent as that gentle expletive "By George!" The awkward gambols of the heroes and heroines of carnival in the fifth act of *An Evening's Love* may be a little hoydenish, but Dryden might justly complain that Collier had misreported him. In the play, Wildblood is making a racket in the dark, and pretending to be one of a troop of evil spirits; he sneezes, and Bellamy, reassured by this evidence of his humanity, smartly calls out, "One of the devils, I warrant you, has got a cold, with being so long out of the fire." The idea is rather funny, and the joke mild enough, surely, to have emanated from an archbishop. To complain that the sentiments of Dorax are atheistical is still more maladroit. Dorax is a renegade Portuguese Catholic, who has sought a home among the Moors. The whole play runs on the tragical result of his desperate sentiments and unbridled godlessness. It is absolutely needful that he should express himself as an atheist, and he cannot be said to do so in any scandalous or needless fashion. As well might Collier have demanded that, in the tragedy of Sophocles, Ajax should always be fawning on the gods. The charge against Congreve, that Valentine says "I am Truth," is more frivolous still, because all that can be urged against it is that it may be conceived to contain one of those reminiscences of Biblical phraseology which have formed one of the charms of the secular style of so many English authors. Collier should have been aware that this particular class of charges is one which it is difficult to bring home. He should have contented himself with the limited number of distinctly profane burlesquings of Scripture which he was able to find, and not have weakened his argument by objecting to much that was not objectionable to any healthy conscience.

He becomes very funny in his third chapter, "The Clergy abus'd by the Stage;" for he forms a strange conception of what "clergy" are. He defines the body as consisting of all those who make religion their profession, whether their religion be true or false. To an old Tory like Collier, the Dissenters seemed despicable, and scarcely held within the general bounds of Christianity. But his dignity is as much wounded by discovering that "the *Old Bachelor* has a throw at the dissenting ministers," as he is by reading Horner's maxim, "your Churchman is your greatest Atheist." He even takes the gods of the Egyptians under his protection, and cannot forgive Dryden for allowing his Greek lady in *Cleomenes* to rail against Apis, "accurs'd be thou, grass-eating, ſoddered God!" which he very oddly and obliquely takes to be "a handsome compliment to libertines;" and censures with absurd gravity Lee's rant about striking the gods "deaf with everlasting peals of thundering joy." He quotes a great many things of this nature, and then turns to show that the tragedians of antiquity treated their gods and their priests with more respect; that Virgil, when he draws a minister of religion, paints him "all gold, purple, scarlet, and embroidery, and as rich as nature, art, and rhetoric can make him." The real reason of all this presently appears, when Collier naïvely complains that the modern poets do not treat clergymen "like persons of condition." He is more sensible, indeed he is wholly right, when he says that Christianity is no proper subject for fooling, and that the holy function is too solemn a thing to be sported with by loose actors in a play-house. He would have said this to more purpose if he had kept to the true religion, and if he had not been so solicitous about the personal dignity of the cloth.

In his fourth chapter, Collier charges the dramatists with making their principal characters vicious, and then rewarding them at the close of the play. On this subject he writes extremely well, and the poets were an easy prey to his sarcasm. He is particularly active in taking Congreve to task, and arraigns the heroes of each of that poet's comedies as profligate debauchees. Sometimes it is difficult to see what possible defence there could be; as, for example, when, taking *The Old Bachelor*, he points out how degrading are the whole character and action of Harcourt. Dryden had answered a similar charge in the preface to *An Evening's Love;* this play was specially hateful to Collier, and he takes up Dryden's specious arguments one by one, and answers them. He now goes away a little from his main line of attack, and scourges that absurd inflated rant, which was a veritable disease of the tragedy of his time. In this connection he makes a pun, or joke, which may be taken as a specimen of his humour. Celadea, in *Love Triumphant*, "a maiden lady, who is afraid her spark will be married to another," shouts out to Nature to pull the fabric of the globe about their ears, "and make a Chaos." Collier says that instead of calling for a chaos she would do much better to cal for a chair, trip off in it, and keep her folly to herself. He closes this chapter with a protest against the treating of people of quality cavalierly on the stage. By this he does not, as might be supposed, mean the satirizing of real persons of rank under feigned names, but the giving titles of nobility to fictitious persons who are to be represented in ridiculous situations. He remarks, in carrying out this idea, that Molière never ventures to fly his satire at any one higher than a marquis. The inference is not well founded; *La Comtesse d' Escarbagnas*, for example, is full of the aristocracy from beginning to end. In any case it is difficult to see the force of the remark, nor why marquises should be abandoned to the gaiety of nations.

Here Collier should have finished his book, and here in all probability it did at one time close. Hitherto most of his allusions have been to plays in general, and he has gone hither and thither over the beds of gaudy stage-flowers collecting his bag of poisonous honey. He has, by this time, made all his points and expended the best part of his wit and invective; but he seems unwilling to leave off, and he breaks into what is really an appendix, a review of four special plays, the *Amphitryon* and the *King Arthur* of Dryden, D'Urfey's *Don Quixote* and Vanbrugh's *Relapse*. On the subject of these dramas he has no very unexampled remarks to make, and as they contain nothing bearing in any way on Congreve, it is not needful to discuss them here. Collier has not the slightest difficulty in proving the veteran Dryden and the new, brilliant, uncompromising Vanbrugh guilty of an infinite number of breaches of decorum. What is more surprising is that he should have thought it worth while to criticise Tom D'Urfey's twentieth play, when the nineteen that preceded it did but combine to prove him a scurrilous and witless buffoon, on whose shoulder the king might lean to hum over a song, but whom it was needless to discuss in any grave examination of British dramatic literature. Collier has not yet closed. He has a final chapter dealing with the opinions expressed regarding the stage by grave Pagan authorities, by the English Church, and by the English State. Of these the first is wholly unimportant, and led the critic into pedantic disquisitions which laid him open to counter attack. What could it matter, when Congreve and Vanbrugh were arraigned at the bar of decency, whether Xenophon commended the Persians because they would not "so much as suffer their youth to hear anything that's amorous or tawdry," or whether Tacitus blamed Nero for "hiring decayed gentlemen for the stage"? Indeed, this portion of the *Short View* would be very flat, if it were not for a singularly nimble passage, in which Collier adroitly makes a personage of Wycherley's give very valuable evidence on the Puritan side. He draws himself together, moreover, for some vigorous concluding pages, in which he sums up his arraignment of the modern theatre in language which is exceedingly forcible and appropriate.

What event it was that excited Collier to the composition of the *Short View* does not seem to be known. After having meditated on the subject for many months, he suddenly developed his attack. Dennis tells us that the volume "was conceived, disposed, transcribed, and printed in a month," and though the preface is dated March 5, 1698, it was issued only a few days later. The sensation which it caused was unparalleled. No purely literary event—not even the publication of *Absolom and Achitophel*, which was not purely literary—had awakened anything like so great an excitement since the Restoration. The book sold like wild-fire, and it may be interesting to note, from more than one source, that Collier was paid £50 for the first edition. For the next twelve months the town was convulsed with pamphleteers attacking and defending the *Short View*, sometimes in books longer than the original. In 1699 the controversy began to slacken, but the fire of answering pamphlets went sullenly on for many years, nor can properly be said to have closed until William Law brought the whole controversy to a climax, in 1726, with his *Absolute Unlawfulness of the Stage Entertainment fully demonstrated.* The eagerness with which the discussion which Collier had so courageously raised was taken up was in itself a proof of the timeliness of his attack. It was, indeed, only too timely; it did not merely cure the disease, it presently killed the patient also. For the moment, however, the drama was found to have many friends, and of the most important of these an account will now be given, chronologically arranged for the first time, and critically examined.

For some weeks, though much was said, nothing was printed. There were no weekly newspapers under William III. to ventilate a literary quarrel rapidly. It was in the course of the month of April, that the anonymous tragedy of *Phaeton* appeared, advertized on its title-page to contain "Some Reflections on a Book called a Short View." This tragedy was the second produced by a young and active poetaster, Charles Gildon, who drew a venal quill long afterwards in the days of Pope, but who, under Dryden, was almost respectable. The "Reflections," evidently added after everything else was in type as an appendix to the preface, only extend to two pages and a half. Gildon calls Collier "our younger Histrio-Mastix," and he sympathises confidentially with Mr. Congreve and "Mr. Vanbrook," but is careful to express no word of sympathy with Dryden. He admits frankly enough that the stage is corrupt, and stands in great need of reform, but declares that Collier has exaggerated the evil, and has alienated sympathy by the brutality of his tone. Gildon, as befitted a prominent dramatic critic and aspiring tragic playwright, is enthusiastic about the art of the theatre, and his last words are, "The wit of man can invent no way so efficacious as Dramatic Poetry to advance virtue and wisdom, and the supreme duty of an Englishman, . . . the love of our country." In two plays which shortly followed, in *The Campaigners* of D'Urfey, and in the *Beauty in Distress* of Motteux, Collier is rudely handled, but without wit or force.

Gildon promised that when he had leisure he would write *A Vindication of the Stage.* The very interesting tract, however, which was published under that title on the 17th of May,[1] is from a very different, and, no doubt, a far more accomplished hand than his. There exists, I believe, not even a tradition which connects this pamphlet with any known name. I have little hesitation, however, in attributing it to Wycherley. It is the freshest and most vivacious of all the replies to Collier, although not the most weighty. It is written from the country, and it tells the reader that the *Short View* has "made a great noise with us in Staffordshire." At this time Wycherley was living at Cleve, in Shropshire, and without forcing the allusion it may be suggested that he was near enough to Staffordshire to judge of the effect of the attack on Congreve's country neighbours, and yet did not choose to mention his own particular county. What further tends to confirm the idea is that the author defends Congreve,

[1] The "Post-Man."

but mentions no one else. Wycherley would not, of course, in a pamphlet kept studiously anonymous, mention himself, nor would he feel called upon to defend Vanbrugh, a young man who had come to the front since his own retirement, while Congreve was one of his particular friends. The *Vindication* is both gay and graceful; it quotes George Herbert and Sir William Temple in defence of the stage, and it teases Collier quite roguishly about his lumbering display of classic learning. It goes into no critical particulars, defends no special passages, and, in fact, skirmishes around the subject very lightly, but without doing much damage. There is something about the tone of the pamphlet, and the way in which Congreve's name is introduced, which makes me think it was intended that Congreve should be supposed to be the writer. This, perhaps, is the real meaning of the Staffordshire reference.

The next champion of the stage was a foolish and voluble creature, Edward Filmer, a retired Oxford don of good family, now between fifty and sixty years of age, who in 1697 had come forward for the first and only time as a playwright, with a very insipid tragedy of *The Unnatural Brother*. Filmer thought that this experience gave him a right to discourse on theatrical matters, and to become a frequent defender of the stage for the next nine years. His first treatise, an anonymous volume of 118 pages, was published on the 26th of May.[1] It is remarkable mainly for its insufferable style, fulsome and ornate, and for the candour with which it treats Collier. The tempers of the combatants were even yet not fully

[1] The "Post-Man."

roused, and in this his earliest book Filmer can speak of the degree to which "Wit and learning shine through [Collier's] whole piece." Filmer's exact title is *A Defence of Dramatic Poetry.* His principal argument is directed against Collier's unhappy appeal to ancient drama, and when Filmer has shown the Greeks and Romans to have written obscenely, he thinks the whole difficulty is settled.

A week later, on the 6th of June,[1] a much more serious writer than any of the above came forward in the person of John Dennis, with his tract on *The Usefulness of the Stage.* Dennis was at this time at the height of his powers, unsoured by disappointment, untainted by envy; he was really, on a question of literary art, a very formidable opponent. He opens in an admirable tone:—

> If Mr. Collier had only attacked the corruptions of the stage, I should have been so far from blaming him that I should have publicly returned him my thanks; for the abuses are so great that there is a necessity for the reforming them. . . . No man can make any reasonable defence either for the immorality or the immodesty or the unnecessary wanton profaneness which are too justly urged upon [the English stage].

Nor will Dennis defend particular gentlemen, who, he doubts not, will, if they have anything to say, take an early opportunity of saying it. But he has to protest against two things, against Collier's unfairness, his habit of wresting phrases and expressions out of their proper meaning and intention, and against his uncompromising brutality of tone. Dennis remarks with dignity, and the

[1] The "Post-Man."

rebuke was not unneeded, "He has given them [*i.e.*, the dramatists] some language which must be resented by all who profess humanity." But this was an appeal to a side upon which the sensibilities of the Puritan critic were impregnable.

Dennis undertakes a warm defence of Wycherley. Of Congreve he does not say a word, partly, no doubt, because Congreve was now supposed to be engaged on a reply of his own. He divides his homily into three parts, and endeavours to prove that the stage is useful in conducing to the happiness of mankind, in supporting government, and in assisting religion. He is little occupied in defending particular plays or the conduct of the existing dramatists, but he foresees the damage which will be done to the stage in general if the contagion of Collier's Puritanism spreads, and he warmly deprecates the exaggeration which kills the patient in the endeavour or pretence to cure him. This little book of Dennis is the most serious of the crowd of replies which Collier's attack called forth.

Two days after the publication of Dennis' *Usefulness of the Stage*,[1] there appeared *A Short Vindication of the Relapse and the Provok'd Wife, by the Author.* Scarcely a year had elapsed, since this vigorous contributor to the drama had first made his appearance, and he was already the writer of three very successful plays. He had been persistently anonymous, and his name was unknown to the public. The buyer of the copy of *A Short Vindication* in my own collection has written "by Captain Vanbrug" across the title-page, and this, rather than the

[1] June 8th, "Flying Post."

now customary "Vanborough," seems to have been the current pronunciation of his name. John Vanbrugh was four years Congreve's senior, and had taken up theatrical interests at the age of thirty, after a wild life in the army. His training, his reckless vehemence of animal spirits, his soldierly habits, all prepared him to put the finishing touch on the debauchery of the stage; and it would be idle to attempt to deny that Vanbrugh, who is one of the merriest and most ingenious of comic writers, is also one of the most ribald. The *Relapse* and the *Provok'd Wife* had awakened Collier's extreme displeasure, and he was more blind to the artistic merit of Vanbrugh than to that of any other playwright. He had condemned him utterly and scurrilously, and the town looked to the gallant captain for a reply. The poet's first intention had been to take no notice. His friends, "the righteous as well as the unrighteous," assured him that the attack which Collier had made was not likely to injure him, and persuaded Vanbrugh to disdain it. But the sensation the *Short View* had caused increased instead of passing away; "this lampoon," says Vanbrugh in June, "has got credit enough in some places to brand the persons it mentions" with a bad reputation, and he thinks it "now a thing no farther to be laughed at."

Vanbrugh does not answer with a very good grace, for, indeed, he had not much to say. He makes a few points. He is particularly happy in exposing Collier's blunder in charging the poet with profanity for putting in Lord Foppington's mouth expressions which, from the lips of such a man, are plainly compliments to the Church which he seems to attack. It is not less plain that the most dutiful comedian in the world need not blush to have allowed a nurse to call an intriguing chaplain "a wicked man." The use of such phrases as "thou angel of light," "Providence takes care of men of merit," is shown to be wholly conventional and innocent, and on the last pages of his *Short Vindication*, Vanbrugh takes a certainly very unfortunate criticism of Collier's on a passage in the *Relapse*, and turns upon it with such an impudent and happy adroitness, that he leaves his reader in the best of humours, and his adversary superficially discomfited.

Vanbrugh's reply, however, comes, on the whole, to very little. It mollifies the wounds which *A Short View* had made, it brushes off a little of the mud, straightens a little the ruffled garments of the two outraged plays, makes the poet's personal position a little more endurable, but does nothing whatever to disprove on broad lines Collier's general indictment. Of any one but himself, Vanbrugh judiciously says nothing, but declares that he was helped in writing the *Relapse*, by a gentleman who has "gone away with the Czar, who has made him Poet Laureate of Muscovy." This statement does not appear to have been noted by any writer on Vanbrugh, nor am I able to conjecture what gentleman the poet alludes to.

Edward Filmer had been in so great a hurry to address the public that he had not said half that he intended in his first pamphlet. On the 23rd of June,[1] therefore, he issued *A Further Defence of Dramatic Poetry*, a treatise in the same affected, alembicated style, which would be

[1] The "Post Boy."

totally without value did it not happen to contain this interesting passage :

> It goes for current authority round the whole town that Mr. Dryden himself publicly declared [the *Short View*] unanswerable, and thanked Mr. Collier for the just correction he had given him ; and that Mr. Congreve and some other great authors had made much the same declaration ; which is all so notoriously false, so egregious a lie, that Mr. Dryden particularly always looked upon it as a pile of malice, ill-nature, and uncharitableness, and all drawn upon the rack of wit and invention.

Filmer is principally occupied in the *Further Defence* with defending the *Relapse*, his tract being evidently written before Vanbrugh's *Short Vindication* appeared.

It was now grown to be four months since Collier had put his ram's horn to his lips. Instead of dying away, the echoes had gathered volume, and the play-houses were ringing with them. The only successful new play of the season had been Catharine Trotter's *Fatal Friendship*, in which great decorum and modesty of speech had been preserved. Betterton and Mrs. Bracegirdle had been fined for profane language. Narcissus Luttrel tells us that on May 12, 1698, "The Justices of Middlesex did not only prosecute the play-houses, but also Mr. Congreve for writing the *Double Dealer*, D'Urfey for *Don Quixote*, and Tonson and Brisco, booksellers, for printing them ; and that women frequenting the play-houses in masks tended much to debauchery and immorality." The theatres were awed, at all events for the moment ; play-goers had a novel sense of the awakening conscience. But the desire to hear what the leaders of dramatic literature had to say was extreme, and this curiosity centred around Congreve, whose position at Lincoln's Inn Theatre, as well as his rank as a poet, made him, rather than the retired Dryden, the playwright of the age *par excellence.* Long obstinately silent, the author of *Love for Love* gave way at last, not because he had anything to say, but because public opinion obliged him to reply. He relinquished his stronghold of disdainful silence, and not having answered at once, he had the want of tact to reply when temper had become acerbated, when interest was dulled, and when the obvious repartees had been already made by less witty men. All eyes were upon him, he strained his powers to the full, and he collapsed in a failure which is distressing to contemplate after nearly two hundred years. Congreve was incomparably the cleverest man who engaged in the Collier controversy, and yet his contribution to it is perhaps the least fortunate, as it certainly is the least decorous of all.

His book, for it is more than a pamphlet, appeared on the 12th of July,[1] under the title *Amendments of Mr. Collier's False and Imperfect Citations*, with imposing mottoes on the title-page from Martial and Sallust. Congreve says that he has "been taxed of laziness, and too much security" in so long neglecting to vindicate himself. He at once plunges into his task, and he takes up a position which none of his predecessors had ventured to assume. Gildon and Dennis had admitted that reform was called for; even Vanbrugh had not attempted to declare that there was no truth in Collier's general accusation. But Congreve dares to do this. He declares that "the greater

[1] The "Post Boy."

part of those examples which [Mr. Collier] has produced are only demonstrations of his own impurity, they only savour of his utterance, and were sweet enough till tainted by his breath." This is a fair example of the unlucky mode in which Congreve undertakes his own defence; he attempts by mere swashbuckler assertions to throw dust in his assailant's eyes. He charges Collier with wanton misrepresentation of his citations, and he offers to "remove them from his dunghill and replant them in the field of nature." It was the game of bluff, a bold stroke, but not justified by success; it was, in fact, extremely injudicious.

The serious part of Congreve's argument may thus be summarized. He says, that Aristotle's definition of comedy lays down that art to be "an imitation of the worse sort of people," in which men are to be laughed out of their vices by ridicule, and the public both warned and diverted at their expense. If the stage were to be so mealy-mouthed as never to permit itself an immodest phrase or a vicious action, the picture of an evil life would be a false one, and would moreover have nothing in it of which the audience could be taught to be ashamed. He says the comic poet, judged by Collier's standard, is first blamed for drawing his satirized characters with ugly faces, and then is told that those faces are evidently the copy of his own. He then passes in detailed review those passages from his own four plays which Collier had specially objected to, and his attempt is to show that the critic, by isolating them from their natural context, had done their meaning and Congreve's intention a great injustice. He says, and the remark is very well founded, that "Collier's vanity in pretending to criticism has extremely betrayed his ignorance in the art of poetry." All these remarks are excellent in their way, and there is material scattered over the *Amendments* enough to have supplied a wiser, and less choleric, controversialist with the framework of a tilting attack. But Congreve is coarsely angry; the playwrights complained that Collier's language was brutal, but Congreve says things about Collier that make the reader blush. In the whole of the unfortunate little volume the most suggestive page is that with which it closes:—

> Is there in the world a climate more uncertain than our own? And, which is a natural consequence, is there anywhere a people more unsteady, more apt to discontent, more saturnine, dark and melancholic than ourselves? Are we not of all people the most unfit to be alone, and most unsafe to be trusted with ourselves? Are there not more self-murderers and melancholic lunatics in England, heard of in one year, than in a great part of Europe besides? From whence are all our sects, schisms, and innumerable subdivisions in religion? Whence our plots, conspiracies, and seditions? Who are the authors and contrivers of these things? Not they who frequent the theatres and concerts of music. No, if they had, it may be Mr. Collier's invective had not been levelled that way; his Gunpowder Treason Plot upon music and plays (for he says music is as dangerous as gunpowder) had broke out in another place, and all his false witnesses had been summoned elsewhere.

It was a serious disaster for comedy in this country that its greatest living representative should meet so serious an attack as that of Collier's in a spirit so frivolous and so violent, and in a manner so thoroughly inadequate. Congreve's position was a difficult one, no doubt; but if he had faced the difficulty with candour and with tact, he might have secured a victory, if not for himself, at least for dramatic literature. As it was, the *Amendments* dealt a fresh blow at the very theatrical party which its aim was to revenge.

Congreve was too amiable and too prosperous a man not to have enemies. The tracts which appeared in the autumn of 1698, purporting to be on Collier's side, are mainly personal attacks on the successful author of *The Mourning Bride*. On the 2nd of September[1] was issued *A Letter to Mr. Congreve on his pretended Amendments*, a very poor performance, in which we are told that Dennis sat solemnly in his club to impeach Collier, which perhaps reflects the importance of the theme as a topic of coffee-house gossip. This was followed by a pamphlet of *Animadversions* on Congreve's *Amendments*, in a dialogue between Mr. Smith and Mr. Johnson, published on the 8th of September,[2] which was one of those wretched productions, inspired by scurrilous personality, from which a biographer borrows material which he is obliged to turn inside out before he uses it. The *Animadversions*, none the less, contain individual touches, which, in the paucity of personal tradition about Congreve, are precious. The character which the poet enjoyed for urbanity and sweetness of disposition is confirmed by the very evidence of this enemy, who by his constant ironical references proves what the general testimony was. "This," he cries, with elaborate sarcasm, "this is your friend, the courteous, the obliging Mr. Congreve, the very pink of courtesy, nay, the very reflection of heaven in a pond."

[1] The "Post-Man." [2] The "Flying Post."

The anonymous writer affects no great virtue in his attack; he admits that he holds a brief for one Mr. P——, who has lately had a play acted at the rival theatre. According to this writer, who is probably identical with the offended playwright, Congreve in his semi-managerial capacity objected to that drama, which nevertheless succeeded. All this gives us material for the almost certain conjecture that the playwright was George Powell, the actor. He was a man of intemperate and factious disposition; he had lately brought out at Drury Lane a comedy of *The Imposture Defeated*, which Mary Pix, who was Congreve's favourite, and one of the Lincoln's Inn dramatists, had openly declared was stolen from a play of hers. No doubt Congreve agreed with her, and had spoken his mind about Powell, who though an excellent, if capricious actor, was a very bad writer. We find, at all events, in the *Animadversions*, this graphic sketch at the rival theatre :—

When in the end, at the representation of this play of my friend's, Mr. Congreve was seen very gravely with his hat over his eyes among his chief actors and actresses, together with the two she-things called Poetesses [no doubt, Mary Pix and Catharine Trotter[1]

[1] This beautiful and ingenious young woman, already a celebrity at eighteen, had written a very complimentary copy of verses on the performance of *The Mourning Bride*. Her best play, *Fatal Friendship*, was brought out at Lincoln's Inn Fields, in 1698, when Congreve was paramount at that theatre, and through life he retained a warm regard for Mrs. Trotter (Mrs. Cockburne). In Dr. Birch's edition of her works, there are two very courteous letters from Congreve to her: the first thanking her for some congratulatory verses on *The Mourning Bride*, and promising to befriend her first play; the second, dated Nov. 2, 1703, returning the MS. of her tragedy of *Revolution in Sweden*, with critical comments.

are meant], which write for his house, as 'tis nobly called; thus seated in state among those and some other of his ingenious critical friends, they fell all together upon a full cry of damnation, but when they found the malicious hiss would not take, this very generous, obliging Mr. Congreve, was heard to say, "We'll find out a new way for this spark, take my word there is a way of clapping of a play down."

The habit of sitting with his hat drawn down over his eyes seems to have been characteristic of Congreve; it is mentioned several times in contemporary pamphlets, and the author of the *Animadversions* in another place says:—

If that be Mr. Congreve's opinion, he need not covet to go to heaven at all, but to stay and ogle his dear Bracilla [Mrs. Bracegirdle] with sneaking looks under his hat, in the little side-box.

The pamphlet opens with a rough sort of poem, attacking Dennis, Hopkins, Mrs. Pix, D'Urfey, Vanbrugh, and Gildon, but with not a word about Congreve. The prose, however, makes up for the reserve of the verse; it is almost entirely a rude attack on Congreve, whom it charges with having become exalted and dictatorial in his success. It is a lewd and scurril piece from which one is almost ashamed to borrow these scraps of biography.

Eight days later[1] appeared a considerable volume, on Collier's side, entitled *The Stage Condemn'd.* The anonymous author of this book, whose name I have not traced,[2] brings together a good deal of curious informa-

[1] The "Flying Post."

[2] The author of *The Stage Acquitted* says that *The Stage Condemn'd* was written by "Mr. R——th, the formidable author of a scandalous newspaper, and the wretched retailer of mad Prynne's enthusiastic cant."

tion, with regard to Charles I.'s Sunday masques, the Sports of the early royalists, and in particular the objections to the stage formulated by the Christian Fathers. He goes minutely into the arguments which had been brought forward by Filmer, Motteux, and Dennis, and examines one or two recent plays. It is a very dull work, and must, one would suppose, have annoyed Collier, who was at this time preparing his forces to fall upon his enemies hip and thigh. If any one doubts the ability of the *Short View*, he has but to compare it with *The Stage Condemn'd*.

It would have been wise in Collier to have rested content with the far-reaching sensation which his original book had caused. Self-respect, perhaps, and judgment certainly, called upon him to take the buffetings of his enemies in silence. He was, however, not the sort of man who likes to serve by standing and waiting. He loved the scent of battle, and on the 10th of November,[1] 1698 (1699 on the title-page), he plunged into the fray with *A Defence of the Short View*. In his preface he announces that he will answer Congreve and Vanbrugh, but will not deign to notice the smaller fry. He has easy work in dealing with Congreve, and is notably and surprisingly superior in wit, on this occasion, to the wittiest of English writers. But he, also, has lost his temper. He is often not witty or judicious at all, but only rude, as when he quotes the description of the drowning Osmyn in *The Mourning Bride*:—

> Pale and expiring, drenched in briny waves,
> God-like even then,

[1] The "Post-Man."

and adds :—

> Death and paleness are strong resemblances of a Deity! But I perceive, to some people, a seraphim and a drowned rat are just alike.

Congreve mainly occupies him; after treating Vanbrugh, he dedicates a final page or two to Dennis and Filmer. He makes no allusion to his awkward lieutenant, the author of *The Stage Condemn'd.* On the whole Collier's *Defence* is not worth reading; it adds nothing of strength to the position captured by the *Short View*, and displays a more arrogant and inartistic temper. On the 6th of December [1] an anonymous hand published *Some Remarks* on Collier's *Defence;* this is very poor, but contends that Collier's dislike for Congreve is founded on that poet's known love of Queen Mary, and partiality for the House of Orange, a suggestion which has a certain plausible novelty. With this tract the first and notable series of controversial publications on the subject of the Immorality of the Stage closes.

On the mind of any one who has been reading through the record of a controversy of this kind, there must always remain a sense of ardour misapplied, of blows given and taken in the dark, of magisterial weakness arraigning a strong culprit, who ascends the bench only in his turn to lose his force and insight. Neither on Collier's side nor on the side of the playwrights was the full truth told; it was certainly not told in love by Collier, nor in wisdom by Congreve. The Puritan, however, was nearer to a genuine discovery than he knew or could

[1] The "Post-Man."

fully make articulate. He was dimly conscious of evil deeds made glorious, of evil words sanctified to the service of the Muses. He dashed in, deeply inspired by a genuine zeal for righteousness; he broke the idols and stamped upon the relics of the poets, nor did he select with care what images he would wreak his vengeance upon. If he had possessed more artistic feeling, it would probably have balked his zeal. There can be no reasonable doubt that he was perfectly honest and God-fearing in his intentions. There can be equally little question that however the poets might quibble about separate passages, they had, indeed, become scandalously licentious in their view of imaginative life, and after this blast of indignant Puritanism the stage had no alternative but speedily to purge itself.

The attitude of Dryden in all this is obscure. Scarcely any of the polemical tracts offer any comment upon the vehement attacks which Collier had made upon Dryden, and the legends of his own opinion on those attacks are inconsistent. Probably he vacillated, and still more probably, having retired from the stage, and being occupied with other work, busy and old, he did not take very much notice. In an epistle to Motteux, on the publication of his *Beauty in Distress*, in June, 1698, Dryden grumbles, but admits some offence in his own writings. A year later, in the preface to the *Fables*, he surrendered the point with indifference, and with a certain contemptuous indolence. In *Cymon and Iphigenia*, on the other hand, he attacks Collier very sharply, and says:—

> In malice witty, and with venom fraught,
> He makes me speak the things I never thought, . . .
> Ill suits his cloth the praise of railing well.

Finally, in the very latest appearance which Dryden made, in the epilogue to the *Pilgrim*, he sums up the whole matter in lines which certainly form the best summary of the Collier controversy:—

> Perhaps the Parson stretched a point too far,
> When with our theatres he waged a war;
> He tells you that this very moral age
> Received the first infection from the stage,
> But sure a banished court, with lewdness fraught,
> The seeds of open vice returning brought.

It was easy to scold the poets, but if the race of theatre-goers, the courtiers and the class who loved to follow and toady them, had not indicated the sort of pabulum they craved, the poets would never have dared so openly to worship the naked Venus of Whitehall.

The century closes in depression of the literary class, and in scathing Puritanical criticism of the poets. But even this dark cloud has its bright side. It does not seem to have been noticed that never in the history of our literature were the leading imaginative writers of the country more united in friendship, more loyal to one another, than during these closing years of the seventeenth century. The aged Dryden and the young Congreve, Wycherley and Southerne, Dennis and Addison and Vanbrugh, men of diverse age and temper, engaged in competition with one another in the most difficult and invidious of professions, are found apparently without mutual suspicion, happily devoted to their business of literature, and expressing for one another an admiration which has all the appearance of a genuine feeling. In 1680, the literary world was torn with envy and jealousy; in 1715, the elements of discord had broken out again. But Collier's attack seemed, while it lasted, to have the effect of silencing petty discords and of sealing among the poets themselves the bonds of personal affection.

CHAPTER IV.

AFTER all this storm and stress, a great calm seems to have fallen on Congreve. During the year 1699 we scarcely catch sight of him at all. He was doubtless occupied in strengthening and encouraging the Lincoln's Inn Theatre, to which he seems to have acted in some measure as manager. The play-houses suffered severely from the popular dislike which resulted from Collier's exposure; and both Tom Brown and Wright tell us how wretched business was throughout 1699, and what low tricks had to be employed to tempt people to come to the theatre. On the 18th of February, 1699, Peregrine Bertie, the King's Chamberlain, sent an order to both play-houses, calling the attention of the actors to the profane and indecent expressions often used in plays, and warning them to use such phrases no more, at their peril. In consequence, when Congreve's *Double Dealer* was revived on the 4th of March, these words were printed on the bills: "Written by Mr. Congreve; with several expressions omitted." In a letter to Mrs. Steward, Dryden notes this circumstance, and says that it is the first time that an author's name has ever been printed in a play-bill, "at least in England." Meanwhile a very strong writer, Farquhar, the last of the great dramatists, made his appearance with *Love and a Bottle*, and prepared the way for the brief revival of comedy which preceded the final catastrophe. At Lincoln's Inn Fields, at Christmas, 1699, a cast of *Henry IV.*, with Betterton as Falstaff, proved highly popular, and the public began to drop in to the theatres once more.

Congreve had undertaken, if his health permitted, to give Betterton's company a play every year, but three full years divided his *Mourning Bride* from *The Way of the World.* His health, although he was not yet thirty, was very unsatisfactory. Dryden tells Mrs. Steward, on the 7th of November, 1699, that Congreve is ill of the gout at Barnet Wells. The last and, as many critics have believed, the greatest of his comedies appeared, so far as we are able to discover, in the first week of March, 1700. On the 12th of that month Dryden writes to Mrs. Steward, "Congreve's new play has had but moderate success, though it deserves much better." On the 28th of March, according to the "Post Boy," the book of *The Way of the World* was published. When this play was acted, Congreve had but just completed his thirtieth year, and it was therefore at a very early age indeed that he voluntarily took leave of "the loathèd stage." At the same age Terence had only produced the *Andria*, and Molière had done nothing. The work of these great masters of comic character was the result of ripened study of life; Congreve, rushing in on the wave of his wonderful intellectual vivacity, fell back into indolence and languor at the very moment when he should have been preparing himself for the greatest triumphs.

Dennis, as Giles Jacob relates, said "a very fine and a very kind thing" on occasion of our poet's retirement, namely that "Mr. Congreve quitted the stage early, and that Comedy left it with him." Perhaps Dennis was not unwilling to snub the two swaggering playwrights in regimentals, Capt. Vanbrugh and Capt. Farquhar. But we should have known little or nothing of the cause of Congreve's retirement, if he himself, in his customary petulance at criticism, had not told us enough to throw light on the matter. The real reason was that, at first, *The Way of the World* was a comparative failure, and the original edition of the play partly explains why. In the preface, addressed to Ralph, Earl of Montague, indeed, the author declares "that it succeeded on the stage was almost beyond my expectation, for but little of it was prepared for that general taste which seems now to be predominant in the palates of our audience." But the whole tone of the dedication belies these words, and shows the poet anxious to defend himself against his born enemies, the critics, by any species of argument that might come to hand. It is possible that he was predisposed to expect failure, for the prologue, which begins—

> Of those few fools, who with ill stars are cursed,
> Sure scribbling fools, called poets, fare the worst,

is in a fine vein of ill-humour, and contains this fragment of self-description :—

> He [Congreve himself] owns, with toil he wrought the following scenes,
> But if they're naught, ne'er spare him for his pains ;

> Damn him the more, have no commiseration
> For dulness on mature deliberation;
> He swears he'll not resent one hiss'd-off scene,
> Nor, like those peevish wits, his play maintain,
> Who, to assert their sense, your taste arraign;
> Some plot we think he has, and some new thought,
> Some humour, too, no farce, but that's a fault;

and the epilogue, which Mrs. Bracegirdle spoke, seemed to take for granted that the play would be pulled in pieces. In later years, Sir Richard Steele wrote a copy of commendatory verses, afterwards usually prefixed to *The Way of the World*,—verses, by the way, containing that delightful couplet which struck Thackeray as so very comical, in which it is said of Congreve that—

> Implicitly devoted to his fame,
> Well-dressed barbarians know his awful name.

In this poem Steele confesses that the rude spectators knew no sense of Congreve's wit. There grew up a legend that on the first night of *The Way of the World* the poet was so angry at the apathy of the spectators, that he rushed in front and rated them for it; but the story is probably founded on Congreve's notorious inability to bear criticism with equanimity.[1]

[1] I have found the fullest version of this pretended incident in a very rare volume, which I owe to the courtesy of M. James Darmesteter, an anonymous translation of *The Way of the World*, published in Paris, as *Le Train du Monde*, in 1759, with an essay on English comedy prefixed:—"On dit que M. Congreve se trouvant dans la coulisse à la première représentation de cette pièce, s'aperçut qu'on n'en était pas content; ce qui l'ayant mis en fureur, il s'avança sur le théâtre, et pria le parterre de ne pas se fatiguer à censurer un auteur résolu de ne plus s'exposer aux jugemens d'un

Successive critics, seeing, what we must all acknowledge, the incomparable splendour of the dialogue in *The Way of the World*, have not ceased to marvel at the caprice which should render dubious the success of such a masterpiece on its first appearance. But perhaps a closer examination of the play may help us to unravel the apparent mystery. On certain sides, all the praise which has been lavished on the play from Steele and Voltaire down to Mr. Swinburne and Mr. George Meredith is thoroughly deserved. *The Way of the World* is the best-written, the most dazzling, the most intellectually accomplished of all English comedies, perhaps of all the comedies of the world. But it has the defects of the very qualities which make it so brilliant. A perfect comedy does not sparkle so much, is not so exquisitely written, because it needs to advance, to develop. To *The Way of the World* may be applied that very dubious compliment paid by Mrs. Browning to Landor's *Pentameron* that, "were it not for the necessity of getting through a book, some of the pages are too delicious to turn over." The beginning of the third act, the description of Mirabell's feelings in the opening scene, and many other parts of *The Way of the World*, are not to be turned over, but to be re-read until the psychological subtlety of the sentiment, the perfume of the delicately

public ignorant. Un auteur qui ferait anjourd'hui la même chose à Londres verrait pleuvoir sur lui une nuée de pommes et d'oranges de la troisième galerie." In this French version the names of the personages are altered, I do not know why; Mirabell is called Clarendon, Witwood and Petulant are Beauclerc and Strafford, Lady Wishfort is Lady Grenham, and Mrs. Millamant is Mrs. Granville. In other respects it conforms pretty closely to the English text.

chosen phrases, the music of the sentences, have produced their full effect upon the nerves. But, meanwhile, what of the action? The reader dies of a rose in aromatic pain, but the spectator fidgets in his stall, and wishes that the actors and actresses would be doing something. In no play of Congreve's is the literature so consummate, in none is the human interest in movement and surprise so utterly neglected, as in *The Way of the World*. *The Old Bachelor*, itself, is theatrical in comparison. We have slow, elaborate dialogue, spread out like some beautiful endless tapestry, and no action whatever. Nothing happens, nothing moves, positively from one end of *The Way of the World* to the other, and the only reward of the mere spectator is the occasional scene of wittily contrasted dialogue, Millamant pitted against Sir Wilful, Witwoud against Petulant, Lady Wishfort against her maid. With an experienced audience, prepared for an intellectual pleasure, the wit of these polished fragments would no doubt encourage a cultivation of patience through less lively portions of the play, but to spectators coming perfectly fresh to the piece, and expecting rattle and movement, this series of still-life pictures may easily be conceived to be exasperating, especially as the satire contained in them was extremely sharp and direct.

Very slight record has been preserved of the manner in which *The Way of the World* was acted. The only part which seems to have been particularly distinguished was that of Mrs. Leigh in Lady Wishfort. Mrs. Bracegirdle, of course, was made for the part of Millamant, and her appearance in the second act, "with her fan spread, and her streamers out, and a shoal of fools for tenders," was carefully prepared; yet we hear nothing of the effect produced. Mrs. Barry took the disagreeable character of Mrs. Marwood, and Betterton had no special chance for showing his qualities in Fainall. Witwoud and Petulant, who keep some of the scenes alive with their sallies, were Bower and Bowman, and Underhill played Sir Wilful. It is very tantalizing, and quite unaccountable, that no one seems to have preserved any tradition of the acting of this magnificent piece.

In *The Way of the World*, as in *The Old Bachelor*, Congreve essayed a stratagem which Molière tried but once, in *Le Misanthrope*. It is one which is likely to please very much or greatly to annoy. It is the stimulation of curiosity all through the first act, without the introduction of one of the female characters who are described and, as it were, promised to the audience. It is probable that in the case of *The Way of the World* it was hardly a success. The analysis of character and delicate intellectual writing in the first act, devoid as it is of all stage-movement, may possibly have proved very tedious to auditors not subtle enough to enjoy Mirabell's account of the effect which Millamant's faults have upon him, or Witwoud's balanced depreciation of his friend Petulant. Even the mere reader discovers that the whole play brightens up after the entrance of Millamant, and probably that apparition is delayed too long. From this point, to the end of the second act, all scintillates and sparkles; and these are perhaps the most finished pages, for mere wit, in all existing comedy. The dialogue is a little metallic, but it is burnished to the highest perfection; and while one repartee rings against the other, the arena echoes as with shock after shock in a tilting-bout. In comparison with what we had had before Congreve's time that was best—with *The Man of Mode*, for instance, and with *The Country Wife*—the literary work in *The Way of the World* is altogether more polished, the wit more direct and effectual, the art of the comic poet more highly developed. There are fewer square inches of the canvas which the painter has roughly filled in, and neglected to finish; there is more that consciously demands critical admiration, less that can be, in Landor's phrase, pared away.

Why, then, did this marvellous comedy fail to please? Partly, no doubt, on account of its scholarly delicacy, too fine to hold the attention of the pit, and partly also, as we have seen, because of its too elaborate dialogue and absence of action. But there was more than this. Congreve was not merely a comedian, he was a satirist also—*asper jocum tentavit.* He did not spare the susceptibilities of his fine ladies. His Cabal-Night at Lady Wishfort's is the direct original of Sheridan's *School for Scandal;* but in some ways the earlier picture is the more biting, the more disdainful. Without posing as a Timon or a Diogenes, and so becoming himself an object of curious interest, Congreve adopted the cynical tone, and threads the brightly-coloured crowd of social figures with a contemptuous smile upon his lips. When we come to speak of his plays as a whole, we shall revert to this trait, which is highly characteristic of his genius; it is here enough to point out that this peculiar air of careless superiority, which is decidedly annoying to audiences, reaches its climax in the last of Congreve's comedies.

We have spoken with high praise of the end of the second act; but perhaps even this is surpassed in the third act by Lady Wishfort's unparalleled disorder at the sight of her complexion, "an arrant ash-colour, as I'm a person," and her voluble commands to her maid; or, in the fourth act, by the scene in which Millamant walks up and down the room reciting tags from the poets, not noticing Sir Wilful, the country clodpole squire, "ruder than Gothic," who takes the ejaculation, "Natural easy Suckling!" as a description of himself. It is to be noticed, as a proof that this play, in spite of its misfortunes, has made a deep impression on generations of hearers and readers, that it is fuller than any other of Congreve's plays of quotations that have become part of the language. It is from *The Way of the World*, for instance, that we take—"To drink is a Christian diversion unknown to the Turk and the Persian"; while it would be interesting to know whether it is by a pure coincidence that Tennyson, in perhaps the most famous of all his phrases, comes so near to Congreve's "'Tis better to have been left, than never to have been loved."

Two months after the first performance of *The Way of the World* occurred one of those events which form landmarks in literary history, and divide one age from another. On the 1st of May, 1700, Dryden died, and after having lain in state at the College of Physicians for ten days, his body was taken to Westminster Abbey by a great procession of more than a hundred coaches carrying men of quality and wit, among whom we are informed that Congreve attended. The funeral train might have been swelled by his own hearse, for now, at the age of thirty, he had ceased almost as completely as Dryden himself to be a living force in literature. Congreve existed nearly thirty years longer; but the record of those years, although it is necessary to continue it, is empty of great facts, and adds little or nothing to the reputation of the poet. The career of Congreve, properly speaking, is crowded into the seven years between January, 1693, and March, 1700. At the latter date the poet expired, and the gentleman of fashion, the scholar, the silent friend, took his place.

In the autumn of 1700 Congreve went abroad, in company with a certain Jacob and Charles, who may be conjectured to have been Jacob Tonson the publisher and Charles Gildon the critic. There exist at the British Museum a little cluster of letters written by the poet, on this occasion, to Edward Porter and to his wife, the actress. The traveller, who is not known to have ever been abroad before or afterwards, left Dover for Calais in the first week of August, rejoiced, on landing, to find "admirable champagne for twelve pence a quart, and as good Burgundy for 15 pence," and then went on to St. Omer. Six weeks later he had been in Brussels and Antwerp, and had driven through Guelderland—"12 leagues together, with a mad fanatic in a waggon, who preached to me all the way." On the 27th of September he was at Rotterdam. We get no light thrown on the object of this little tour in the Low Countries, but it was probably nothing but pleasure. The correspondence is homely, genial, and slight, written without the slightest affectation. As few of Congreve's letters have been preserved, the following, also written to Edward Porter, but at what date is not known,[1] may be worth quoting:—

SIR,—I am forced to borrow ladies' [curling] paper, but I think it will contain all that I can tell you from this place, which is so much out of the world that nothing but the last great news could have reached it. I have a little tried what solitude and retirement can afford, which are here in perfection. I am now writing to you from before a black mountain nodding over me, and a whole river in cascade, falling so near me that even I can distinctly see it. I can only tell you of the situation I am in, which would be better expressed by Mr. Grace if he were here. I hope all our friends are well, both at Salisbury, and Windsor, where I suppose you spent the last week. Pray, whenever you write to them, give my humble service. I think to go the next week to Mansfield Race, where I am told I shall see all the Country; if I see any of your acquaintance, I will do you right to them. I hope Mrs. Longueville's picture has been well finished.

I am, Dear Sir,
Your most humble Servant,
WILL. CONGREVE.

Ham, near Ashbourne, in Derbyshire.
Between six and seven in the morning, birds singing, jolly breezes whistling, etc.

We should know little or nothing of what happened to Congreve between 1700 and 1710 if it were not for the Keally letters. Scarcely any one of the few memoir-writers of that slack time between the death of Dryden and the development of Pope alludes to the famous comic dramatist, whose retirement, without being marked by any intentional cynicism, seems to have been practically complete. On the 4th of December, 1700,

[1] The postmark is August 21.

Charles Montague was made Lord Halifax, and from this time forth it is probable that Congreve was relieved from monetary anxiety; although it certainly is not until 1706 that we have any authority, in spite of the legend of his wealth which successive writers have fostered, for regarding him as a man of affluent means. The Keally correspondence, which has just been alluded to, is a collection of forty-three letters and notes addressed by Congreve, between the years 1700 and 1712, to his Irish friend Joseph Keally, of Keally Mount, Kilkenny, a relative of Bishop Berkeley. These letters have been printed but once, by George Monck Berkeley, in 1789, in his *Literary Relics;* the text is obviously carelessly copied, "Ponson," for instance, being printed for Tonson, and "Love" for Rowe. The letters are slight and unlaboured, but none the less they are of extreme value to us in realizing the character and condition of the poet. They are mostly occupied with small personal details of fact, and, though simple and affectionate, are not, it must be confessed, the sort of letters which a biographer prefers to use for his stock-pot. The letters in 1700 say more about a certain four-footed Sapho than about her master; it is evident that Congreve was solicitously fond of his dogs. In the summer of 1701 "we are at present in great grief for the death of Sapho; she has left some few orphans, one of which, if it can live, is designed for" Keally. Congreve is at this time living in lodgings in Arundel Street, attended by a single man-servant, who sleeps in the back of the same house.

In March, 1701, Congreve once more approached "the ungrateful stage," though merely with a masque in his hands. A competition in music was instituted, four rival composers performing on successive days in Dorset Garden Theatre. The text for them all was written by Congreve, and was published in quarto form, as *The Judgment of Paris*. The musician who carried away the prize was John Eccles, who had set words of Congreve's to music before. The poet's account of the circumstance is interesting. We have few descriptions of English concerts so early as this. Writing on the 26th of March, Congreve says:—

> I wished particularly for you on Friday last, when Eccles his music for the prize was performed in Dorset Garden, and universally admired. Mr. Finger's is to be to-morrow, and Russel[1] and Weldon's follow in their turn. The latter two, I believe, will not be before Easter. After all have been heard severally, they are all to be heard in one day, in order to a decision; and if you come at all this spring, you may come time enough to hear that. Indeed, I don't think any one place in the world can show such an assembly. The number of performers, besides the verse-singers, was eighty-five. The front of the stage was all built into a concave with deal boards; all which was faced with tin, to increase and throw forwards the sound. It was all hung with sconces of wax-candles, besides the common branches of lights usual in the play-house. The boxes and pit were all thrown into one, so that all sat in common; and the whole was crammed with beauties and beaux, not one scrub being admitted. The place where formerly the music used to play, between the pit and the stage, was turned into White's chocolate-house, the whole family being transplanted thither with chocolate, cooled drinks, ratafia, portico, etc., which everybody that would called for, the entire expense being defrayed by the subscribers. I think truly the whole thing better worth coming to see than the Jubilee. . . . Our friend Venus [Mrs. Bracegirdle] performed to a miracle; so did Mrs. Hodgson in Juno. Mrs. Bowman was not quite so well approved in Pallas.

[1] So in Monck Berkeley, but Congreve obviously wrote Purcell [Daniel].

There is too much of the "old Pindaric way" about *The Judgment of Paris*, which, nevertheless, was much admired for its literary qualities on its first production. The modern critic looks through it vainly searching for a single stanza remarkable enough to be quoted. It was very smoothly written, and smoothness was still enough of a rarity to be noted with pleasure. But the reader who is acquainted with the wild ingenious masques of Ben Jonson, or even with the richly brocaded entertainments of Shirley, will be inclined to look upon *The Judgment of Paris* as poor threadbare stuff.[1]

Something more favourable may be said of the *Ode for St. Cecilia's Day* which Congreve produced for the 22nd of November of the same year, 1701. It was the annual practice from 1687 to 1703, and occasionally afterwards, to have a public musical entertainment on this date, and among the poets who were selected to write the Cecilia ode were at various times Dryden, Oldham, Tate, Shadwell, Addison, and Pope. Jeremiah Clarke, Henry Purcell, Blow, Finger, and other leading composers had written the music; on this occasion it was Congreve's friend, John Eccles, who set the words. In this poem Congreve followed somewhat closely on the earlier of Dryden's two famous odes upon a similar occasion, and Dryden, in lyric art, was a happier master than Cowley crossed with D'Urfey. It seems evident that Collins

[1] The British Museum possesses a MS. of *The Judgment of Paris* with Daniel Purcell's music, and doubtless in his handwriting. This MS. has belonged to Robert Smith, the amateur, and contains a long note in his handwriting which erroneously attributes the masque to the year 1699.

afterwards imitated, while he vastly improved upon, this Pindaric to Harmony, in his more celebrated *Ode on the Passions.* This is a fair specimen of Congreve's lyric :—

Thou only, Goddess, first could tell
The mighty charm in numbers found,
And didst to heavenly minds reveal
The secret force of tuneful sound.
When first Cyllenius formed the lyre,
Thou didst the God inspire ;
When first the vocal shell he strung,
To which the Muses sung ;
Then first the Muses sung ; melodious strains
Apollo played,
And Music first began by thy auspicious aid !
Hark ! hark ! again Urania sings !
Again Apollo strikes the trembling strings !
And see the listening deities around
Attend insatiate, and devour the sound.

A certain sincerity, often lacking in Congreve's occasional verse, is given to this ode by the author's knowledge of music and passionate delight in it.

The Ministry seems to have begun to put forth hints of something definitely to Congreve's advantage at the close of 1702.[1] He says, mysteriously, that great revolu-

[1] In 1701, Catharine Trotter, in dedicating her *Unhappy Penitent* to Halifax, says : "I thus address you not as the sovereign judge of perfection, but as the patron and encourager of all who aspire to it, the no less god-like, though less awful character, which, how eminently your Lordship's, the many who flourish under your auspicious influence are a proof, for if we allow a Congreve to owe your favour to your strictest justice, there are numbers who could find their safety but, with me, in appealing to your goodness." This is not cited as a favourable example of the style of the once-illustrious Female Philosopher.

tions have been going on, "things not to be entrusted to frail paper and packet-boats." On the 12th of February, 1703, he writes to thank Keally for the hint that a Commissioner's place might be going begging. He says that Keally may imagine that if such a post could be procured Congreve would omit no trouble to secure it; but, he continues, "I know it is vain, notwithstanding all the fair promises I have had; for I have not obtained a less matter which I asked for. I must have patience; and I think I have. Of my philosophy I make some use, but, by God, the greatest trial of it is, that I know not how to have the few people that I love as near me as I want." These words, even if they stood alone, which is not the case, would be enough, I think, to puff away that phantom of a splendid young Congreve, overwhelmed with places and emoluments, which Thackeray conjured up. In 1702 he was not rich enough to have those few people whom he loved near him; he was confined to modest lodgings in Arundel Street. He had his one little post at the Hackney Coach Office; he had the fluctuating and slender receipts from his five plays; he had, probably, some little patrimony as well. All told, it was not enough to make him a passably rich man.

In 1703 Congreve prefixed some lines to the third edition of the *Reliquiæ Gethinianæ*, a volume containing the remains of Grace, Lady Gethin, originally published in 1699. These remains were essays on Love, on Friendship, on Gratitude, written by a young woman, the daughter of Sir George Norton. Lady Gethin had died on the 11th of October, 1697, in the twenty-first year of her age. Congreve's lines do not seem to be the expression of personal emotion, but to have been called forth by reading the little, old-fashioned essays. It does not, however, appear to have been noticed that to the very rare first edition of 1699 also Congreve had contributed congratulatory verses,[1] which were never reprinted in his works, though he always repeated those of 1703. The *Reliquiæ* is a very odd little quarto, with ghastly funeral folding-plates; and looks half-a-century at least out of date. It belongs to the same order as Owen Feltham's wiseacre *Resolves*, which Lady Gethin probably imitated.

On the 30th of November, 1703, he took his pen in hand, with quite unusual vivacity, to describe to his Irish friend the result of the famous Hurricane which on the preceding Friday night had caused such consternation throughout the length and breadth of "pale Britannia":—

[1] These are here given, not for their merit, but their rarity:—

> I that hate books, such as come daily out
> By public licence to the reading rout,
> A due religion yet observe to this,
> And here assert, if anything's amiss,
> It can be only the compiler's fault
> Who has ill-drawn the charming author's thought;
> That all was right; her beauteous looks were joined
> To a no less admired excelling mind;
> But oh! this glory of frail nature's dead,
> As I shall be that write, and you that read;
> Once to be out of fashion, I'll conclude
> With something that may tend to public good,—
> I wish that piety, for which in heaven
> The Fair is placed, to the lawn-sleeves were given,
> Her justice to the knot of men whose care
> From the raised millions is to take their share.

Our neighbour in Howard Street [Mrs. Bracegirdle] 'scaped well, though frighted, only the ridge of the house being stripped; and a stack of chimneys in the next house fell luckily into the street. I lost nothing but a casement in my man's chamber, though the chimneys of the Blue Ball continued tumbling by piece-meal most part of the night at Mr. Porter's. The wind came down the little court behind the back parlour, and burst open that door, bolts and all, whirled round the room, and scattered all the prints; which, together with the tables and chairs it mustered into one heap, and made a battery of them to break down the other door into the entry, whither it swept them; yet broke not one pane of the window which joined to the back-court door. It took off the sky-light of the stairs, and did no more damage there.

Most of the theatrical events in Congreve's life took place in the month of March. In February, 1704, we find him anxiously preparing for a performance of which we know little in detail. It was no great matter; it was merely the *Monsieur de Pourceaugnac* of Molière, but it has caused a certain amount of bibliographical mystification. Vanbrugh, Congreve, and Walsh set to work to translate, or rather, probably, to adapt, Molière's farce; each took one act, and the piece was finished in two mornings. As Congreve says: "It was a compliment made to the people of quality at their subscription music, without any design to have it acted or printed further. It made people laugh, and somebody thought it worth his while to translate it again, and print it as it was acted; but if you meet such a thing, I assure you it was none of ours." The "thing" exists in the form of a rare quarto entitled *Monsieur de Pourceaugnac, or Squire Trelooby*, published on the 19th of April, 1704. In the preface to this play the translator says that he had completed and designed it for the English stage, "had he not been prevented by a translation of the same play done by other hands, and presented at the New Play-House the 30th of last month. When I was told the great names concerned in the exhibiting of it to so glorious an assembly, and saw what choice was made of the comedians, . . . I presently resolved upon the publication of it." He goes on to say that the Congreve version was incomplete, and omitted two long scenes ; and tells us that, although the farce proved highly popular, and was much called for in book form, the authors obstinately refused to print it, some scandal having been caused by its performance, "some thinking it was a party-play made on purpose to ridicule the whole body of West-country gentlemen, others averring that it was wrote to expose some eminent doctors of physic in this town."

All this seems clear enough, but there remain difficulties. Vanbrugh, Congreve, and Walsh called their farce *Squire Trelooby;* so does the anonymous translator, who brings the hero, as they did, from Cornwall. Pourceaugnac in the original comes from Limoges, but there is nothing in that to suggest to two independent minds Trelooby and Cornwall. Moreover, the printed play gives the prologue written by Garth and the epilogue spoken by Mrs. Bracegirdle. Now that the former piece was actually spoken seems to be proved by the fact that one couplet in it—

> But if to-day some scandal should appear,
> Let those precise Tartuffes bind o'er Molière—

is elsewhere quoted from memory as having been spoken on the occasion of the 30th of March. Mrs. Bracegirdle's epilogue is anonymous, but it is evidently from the hand of Congreve. It contains such admirably characteristic lines as these :—

> The World by this important project sees
> Confederates can dispatch if once they please,

(referring to the speed with which the three confederated wits had completed their task)

> They show you here what ills attend a life,
> And all for that vexatious whim, a wife,
> What world of woes a wretched wight surround,
> By bantlings baited, and by duns dragooned,
> By bullies bastinadoed, teased by cracks,
> Wheedled by rooks and massacred by quacks.

The bill of the actors' names, too, is the genuine one, and it seems not at all certain, in spite of Congreve's cautious letter to Keally, that this *Squire Trelooby* of 1704 does not virtually represent the play which the joint authors thought it wise to disown. The mystification does not end here. In 1734, when all the persons concerned were dead, Ralph edited and produced at Drury Lane a comedy of *The Cornish Squire*, which he professed to have discovered in the MS. of Vanbrugh, Congreve, and Walsh, and to have altered in various respects. This differs from the *Squire Trelooby* of 1704. Ozell translated *Monsieur de Pourceaugnac*, but his version is supposed to have never been printed. It is possible that what Ralph published under the three more eminent names is really Ozell's version.

Squire Trelooby was very popular. It was first played

on the 30th of March, with "subscription music," by select comedians from both houses. On the 23rd of May it was acted again for "our neighbour" Mrs. Bracegirdle's benefit, and for Mrs. Leigh's benefit on the 6th of June. On the 28th of January, 1706, it was revived as a new piece under Congreve and Vanbrugh's direction. To close this not very important episode, it may be added that the printed version of the play was attributed to Garth, which, if true, would account for the technical accuracy of the long medical dialogue at the close of the first act. We can imagine the three poets appealing to their friend, the author of *The Dispensary*, and declaring that this scene, being beyond their power, "ne demande pas moins qu'un Esculape comme vous, consommé dans vôtre art."

On the 1st of June, 1704, Mrs. Bowman had a benefit of *Love for Love*, for which Congreve wrote a new prologue and a song called "The Misses' Lamentation," in which the ladies deplored their inability to come any longer to first-night performances in vizard masks. This abuse, in fact, had been put a stop to by an edict of Queen Anne, of the 17th of January, 1704, which tightened the cords of discipline about the necks of the theatres in several directions. The reformation of the stage, so courageously started by Collier, was now rapidly developing, in answer to a public demand for cleanliness and sobriety. Congreve during this month was severely punished by the gout, and it is now that we hear for the first time of his going to Bath for the waters. In October we get a slight glimpse of him in a letter to Keally:—

I have a multitude of affairs, having just come to town after nine weeks' absence. I am grown fat, but you know I was born with somewhat of a round belly. . . . Think of me as I am, nothing extenuate. My service to Robin, who would laugh to see me puzzled to buckle my shoe, but I'll fetch it down again.

These read like the playful confessions of an obese but green old age; the writer was only thirty-four years of age at the time. In the same month, after having lost sight of Swift out of Congreve's intimacy since the two men were youths fresh from Ireland, we find chronicled the publication of the *Tale of a Tub*. It is curious to note that Congreve, the younger of the two, had now practically completed his career, and was resting on his laurels, while the elder was making his first important essay in publicity. Keally has not liked Swift's satire, but finds himself, as far as Dublin is concerned, alone in his want of enthusiasm. The cautious and comfortable Congreve has found his old friend's satire equally distasteful:—

I am of your mind as to the Tale of a Tub. I am not alone in the opinion, as you are there; but I am pretty near it, having but very few on my side, but those few are worth a million. However, I have never spoke my sentiments, not caring to contradict a multitude. Bottom[1] admires it, and cannot bear my saying I confess I was diverted with several passages when I read it, but I should not care to read it again. That he thinks not commendation enough.

About this time, very unfortunately for us, there comes a break of a year and a half in the Keally correspondence.

[1] So printed in the Berkeley correspondence; but, appropriate as the name may seem as describing the ordinary appraiser of literature, it is perhaps more likely that on this occasion Congreve wrote "Betterton."

But the year 1705 is precisely that in which we should have particularly chosen, had it been possible, to see what our hero was doing. It was a year of return, in measure, to the publicity of theatrical life. In the winter of 1704 Vanbrugh had become manager of Lincoln's Inn Fields Theatre, and on the 9th of April, 1705, the same poet opened the Queen's Theatre in the Haymarket under the joint management of Congreve and himself.[1] An Italian Pastoral, *The Triumph of Love*, was the first piece produced, and Mrs. Bracegirdle pronounced an epilogue specially composed by Congreve for the occasion. It promised that the bucolic sweetness of the opening night should not too often be repeated :—

> In sweet Italian strains our shepherds sing,
> Of harmless loves our painted forests ring
> In notes, perhaps less foreign than the *thing*.
>
> To sound and show at first we make pretence ;
> In time we may regale you with some sense,
> But that, at present, were too great expense ;

and it ended with what sounds very much like a prediction of a new comedy by Vanbrugh, a declaration that they would soon

> Paint the reverse of what you've seen to-day,
> And in bold strokes the vicious world display.

[1] It does not seem certain that Congreve had hitherto entirely relinquished his share of theatrical management at the other house. In Mr. W. R. Baker's collection of MSS. there is a note from W. Davenant to Tonson, dated from Frankfort, April 20, 1702, in which he says : "Pray give my service to Mr. Congreve and desire him to let me be remembered in the dressing-room at Lincoln's Inn Fields."

This, no doubt, referred to that admirable piece, *The Confederacy.* Congreve is said to have had a share in the new theatre, a share which he relinquished, together with his management, before many months were over.

On the 25th of June, 1705, a novel experiment was tried at the Haymarket theatre, a performance of *Love for Love,* in which all the parts were acted by women. But about this time Congreve's eyesight began to be troublesome; it was a symptom of the general gout which ran through his system. This, there is no question, was the final cause of his retirement from theatrical enterprise. A man crippled by obesity, and threatened with blindness, could undertake no stage-management with any hope of success. In December, 1705, he received a post of very considerable emolument, that of Commissioner of Wine Licenses, and it is now, for the first time, that we can with any confidence think of Congreve as a rich man. "The greater part of the last twenty years of his life," we are told, "was spent in ease and retirement," and although it was not until 1711 that he really became wealthy, he must now, with his Hackney Coaches and his Wines, his little patrimony and the revenue of his five plays, have been more than comfortably provided for.

Two occasional poems belong to the year 1705. One is *The Tears of Amaryllis,* an idyl on the death of the Marquis of Blandford, published in June.[1] It is in the

[1] On the 1st of July, 1705, Congreve wrote to Jacob Tonson in Amsterdam: "Your nephew told me of copies that were dispersed of the Pastoral, and likely to be printed, so we have thought fit to prevent 'em and print it ourselves."—From a note in Mr. W. R. Baker's collection of MSS.

most inflated style of rococo pastoral, adorned with all the customary accessories of rural English landscape, such as tigers and wolves, nymphs and sylvan gods, weeping gums and purple buds and myrtle chaplets. The mother of the young gentleman weeps, and the consequence is that

> Nature herself attentive silence kept,
> And motion seemed suspended while she wept.

It is written, in a wholly false taste, to a Dresden china ideal, but the couplets rush on with a fluent and almost unctuous ease, such as no one else achieved until Pope began to write. If the substance of these occasional poems of Congreve's had been even tolerably real or decently weighty, the curious polish of the form would have saved them. But they were as empty as so many iridescent bubbles.

The other poem of 1705 is occasional also, but this is of far greater merit. The *Ode on Mrs. Arabella Hunt Singing* is one of Congreve's genuine successes. It is a false Pindaric, it is deformed by hideous and ludicrous conceits, but it contains, in its descriptions of the effect of great music on a sympathetic listener, some of the most ingenious interpretations which this situation has called forth :—

> Let all be hushed, each softest motion cease,
> Be every loud tumultuous thought at peace,
> And every ruder gasp of breath
> Be calm, as in the arms of death,
> And thou, most fickle, most uneasy part,
> Thou restless wanderer, my heart,
> Be still ! gently, ah ! gently leave,
> Thou busy, idle thing, to heave !

> Stir not a pulse! and let my blood,
> That turbulent, unruly flood,
> Be softly stayed.
> Let me be, all but my attention, dead.
> Go, rest, unnecessary springs of life,
> Leave your officious toil and strife,
> For I would hear her voice, and try
> If it be possible to die.

It has been noticed that the two last lines of the *Ode on Mrs. Arabella Hunt Singing* seem to have had the honour of haunting the ear of Keats. Congreve writes—

> Wishing for ever in that state to lie,
> For ever to be dying so, yet never die;

while one draft of Keats' last sonnet closes with the couplet—

> Still, still to hear her tender-taken breath,
> And so live ever, or else swoon to death.

Arabella Hunt, who was the most distinguished vocalist of her age, and also a very accomplished performer on the lute, died in December of this same year, 1705. Congreve improvised the following quatrain on the occasion:—

> Were there on earth another Voice like thine,
> Another Hand so blessed with skill divine,
> The late-afflicted world some hopes might have,
> And harmony retrieve thee from the grave.

Few things would be more interesting than to recover a series of intimate memoirs, or a collection of unpublished letters, throwing light on the theatrical life of London during the first decade of the eighteenth century. During this period the theatre underwent revolution upon revolution; still flourishing in appearance, with dolphin-colours, English drama of the literary class was just about to expire, and the modern forms of stage-entertainment were taking its place. Experiment after experiment was tried to win back the exhausted sympathies of the public, and it is precisely at this juncture, when positive information would be so extremely valuable, that we have to fall back upon a few careless pages of Colley Cibber, some casual references in the newspapers, which now first begin to notice the stage, and one or two passing allusions in the correspondence of the day. It appears that the first result of opening the Haymarket theatre had been to exceed the demand for theatrical amusement, and it became impossible to fill all the houses with spectators. The famous school of actors which had risen to its height under William III. had grown old without being strengthened by the accession of adequate youthful talent. Most of the great names that appear on the bills of Congreve's first comedies had now passed out of existence. Betterton himself was over seventy, and yet, old as he was, he had no competitor to fear among the new generation of actors. As Colley Cibber rather pathetically says, in 1706 "these remains of the best set of actors, that I believe were ever known at once in England, by time, death, and the satiety of their hearers, had mouldered to decay."

In April Congreve writes that there is to be a union

of the two houses. Nothing else, it was believed, could recover the sinking prestige of English drama. It was to the advantage of Sir John Vanbrugh that the overtures should come from Drury Lane; but the curious tricks that were played upon him, and the ingenuities of Swiney, are familiar, so far as anything so very mysterious and cryptic can be said to be familiar, to readers of the *Apology*. Congreve seems to have thrown up his share in the management soon after, if not upon, the secret union of the houses, and the spring of 1706 was fraught with great vexation to him. In the autumn of this same year we hear that "the play-houses have undergone another revolution," and that Vanbrugh also has resigned his authority to Swiney. This marks Congreve's final retirement from public life; he becomes an official pluralist, a gentleman of leisure, an immortal raised upon a species of pedestal, serene above the clash of the living literary world. From this time forth, content to be recognized as the first poet of the past age, he descends no more into the arena of practical competition.

He still retained his scholarship and his love of letters, and to the autumn of 1706 belongs a very creditable publication *A Pindaric Ode to the Queen, with a Discourse on the Pindaric Ode.* The *Discourse* is in prose, and is a real contribution to criticism. For half a century English literature had been overrun, as by a noisome parasitic weed, by the false ode of Pindar as it had revealed itself to Cowley in his hasty study of that poet during his exile in Paris. Misconceiving the form of Pindar, and seeing in the elaborate metrical system of that master of technical lyric nothing but an amorphous chain of longs and shorts, cut up into irregular lengths according to the licentious fancy of the poet, Cowley had introduced the horrid kind of ode which delighted the formlessness of the Restoration. Congreve, as we have seen, had known no better than to swell this flood of titular "Pindaricks." But he had now, in his leisure, been reading Pindar, and the error of Cowley became patent to him. He saw that "the character of these late pindarics is a bundle of rambling incoherent thoughts, expressed in a like parcel of irregular stanzas, which also consist of such another complication of disproportioned, uncertain, and perplexed verses and rhymes." He had made a great discovery, and he proceeded to show what the form of a real ode of Pindar is, with its strophe, antistrophe, and epode, a thing as different from Cowley's "horrid or ridiculous caricatures" as a crystal is from a jelly-fish. His essay is brief, but singularly direct and complete, and places him high among the critics of the age. It is rare, indeed, at that period, to find a question of literary workmanship treated simply from the technical point of view, and not obscured by the vain phraseology of the Jesuits. Congreve's appeal to the English poets to return to the pure Greek form of ode was presently recognized by all the best writers, and in particular the two great odes of Gray show how scrupulously faithful that learned lyrist was in his discipleship of Pindar. The pseudo-pindarics went on being written, and are not, indeed, to this day, wholly abandoned by writers who ought to know better, but from 1706 onwards these deformities have been obliged to confess themselves "irregular."

Congreve exemplified his theory of Greek ode-form in two elaborate odes to Queen Anne and to Godolphin. Unfortunately, correctness of technique does not ensure inspiration, and these carefully modulated poems lack the charm of great lyric verse. They are principally interesting as showing, once more, what has hitherto I think been ignored, the influence which Congreve exercised, by his more ambitious lyrical flights, on William Collins. The address to Calliope in the Ode to Queen Mary is remarkably like the "Passions," as like as clay can be to marble. But when the poet proceeds to flatter Queen Anne, and, in a blustering epode, to heap adulations upon Marlborough, there is no longer even an earthy likeness to the later and nobler bard. The Ode to Godolphin makes a brave attempt to emulate the splendour and melody of Pindar, with direct imitation of the celebration by that poet of the Olympic conquerors. But it is to be feared that to Congreve will scarcely be awarded the olive garland in this race with his intrepid forerunner. Scholarship, smoothness of versification, laborious zeal, all these he possesses; but sincerity, the heavenly spark of style, of imagination, these have not descended upon Congreve in his odes. The *Discourse on the Pindaric Ode*, with its attendant strophes, appeared late in 1706, as a folio pamphlet.

On the 13th of October, 1707, Congreve ceased to be a Commissioner for Licensing Hackney Coaches, apparently without receiving, for the present, any equivalent of a different nature. This is doubtless "my loss," at which he thanks Keally for expressing a cordial sympathy. In the same letter (May 12, 1708) he speaks of receiving a legacy of £1000. His health was very poor; "I am pretty well recovered," he says, "of a very severe fit, which has lasted a month. I think to go abroad for air to-morrow." In a letter of about the same time he uses a pleasant phrase that has now an old-world sound about it; "everybody," he tells Keally, "is your servant, but the old gentlewoman is gone to God." From Steele we learn that Congreve was at Newmarket in October, and back in town, laid up with the gout, in November, 1708. On the 7th of April, 1709, "by the desire of several persons of quality," *Love for Love* was played for Betterton's benefit, and Mrs. Bracegirdle, who had practically quitted the stage, came back to play Angelica. This famous performance is described in a well-known *Tatler*. In April of the next year the venerable Betterton passed away, and with him died the dramatic tradition of the seventeenth century. At this point the meagre correspondence of Congreve with Keally overlaps the notices of the former which begin to appear in Swift's letters, and for the future what brief and unsatisfactory glimpses we get of Congreve are mainly given through the medium of Swift. It was in the year 1708 that Congreve became acquainted with Pope, not yet of age, and read with benignant interest the MS. of the *Pastorals*. An old friend of his, William Walsh, who had also been a wise patron of that young poet, passed away in the same year.

The *Journal to Stella* is now our principal source of personal detail regarding Congreve. On the 26th of October, 1710, Swift writes as follows:—

I was to-day to see Mr. Congreve, who is almost blind with cataracts growing on his eyes; and his case is, that he must wait two or three years, until the cataracts are riper, and till he is quite blind, and then he must have them couched; and besides he is never rid of the gout, yet he looks young and fresh, and is as cheerful as ever. He is younger by three years or more[1] than I, and I am twenty years younger than he. He gave me a pain in the great toe, by mentioning the gout.

Next day he joined Congreve and some other friends over a bowl of bad punch in "a blind tavern." They eschewed the punch, but Sir Richard Temple sent for six flasks of his own wine, and the party sat drinking till midnight. Ten days later, Swift dined with Congreve and Vanbrugh at Sir Richard Temple's, when the latter poet was "very civil and cold" about the too-famous goose-pie verses. All this winter of 1710 Congreve turns up ever and anon in the *Journal to Stella*, though seldom in any very graphic or characteristic way. Steele and Prior, Rowe and Addison, appear among his habitual companions, haunting the same taverns and coffee-houses, while Lady Mary Wortley Montagu is henceforward among his intimates.

In December, 1710, Tonson published the *Works* of Congreve in three volumes, adding, what was now for the first time printed, the opera of *Semele*, a long-drawn insipidity in three acts. Whether this lyrical piece was ever acted or no appears to be uncertain; it had not enjoyed that distinction when it was published, although John Eccles, and after-

[1] Swift, as an old Dublin friend, knew better than the gossips. Congreve was, as we now know, three years and two months Swift's junior.

wards Handel composed music for it. There appears to have been a quarrel, or difference of opinion, between Congreve and his publisher, Jacob Tonson, with regard to the manner in which the *Works* of the former were produced.[1] Rowe indited an amusing eclogue called *The Reconciliation between Jacob Tonson and Mr. Congreve*, in which the publisher tells the poet that he cannot exist without him, and offers to set him up a bed in his dining-room, if only he will let byegones be byegones, and dine once more at the printing-office in Bow Street. Congreve is represented as extremely suave and conciliatory under this pathetic appeal.

On the 13th of February, 1711, Swift tells Stella that Congreve has been very ill with the gout, but that, "blind as he is," he has kindly written out a contribution for the benefit of Harrison, Swift's promising young *protégé*. This was a little heraldic story, which appeared in the *Tatler* as well as in Harrison's Miscellany. Three days later Swift was dining with Congreve and with Estcourt, the author of *The Fair Example*. He laughed for hours in their company, but notes that "Congreve's nasty white wine has given me the heartburn." On the 22nd of June there is a very important entry about Con-

[1] The following document, not I think before printed, is found among the Tonson MSS. in the British Museum :—

June 18th, 1710.

I promise to pay to Mr. Congreve or his order the sum of twenty guineas whenever his vollume of poems which I am now printing shall come to be reprinted and at any time he shall demand give him an account what part of this Impression are disposed of.

Witness my hand

JACOB TONSON, Senr.

greve, which appears to have escaped the notice of those who have written about his opulence, and his absolute superiority to the common misfortunes of the poetic race:—

> I saw Will Congreve attending at the Treasury, by order, with his brethren, the Commissioners of the Wine Licences. I had often mentioned him with kindness to the Lord Treasurer; and Congreve told me, that, after they had answered to what they were sent for, my lord called him privately, and spoke to him with great kindness, promising his protection, etc. The poor man said he had been used so ill of late years, he was quite astonished at my lord's goodness, etc., and desired me to tell my lord so; which I did this evening, and recommended him heartily. My lord assured me he esteemed him very much, and would always be kind to him; that what he said was to make Congreve easy, because he knew people talked as if his lordship designed to turn everybody out, and particularly Congreve; which indeed was true, for the poor man told me he apprehended it. As I left my lord Treasurer I called on Congreve, (knowing where he dined), and told him what had passed between my lord and me: so I have made a worthy man easy, and that is a good day's work.

Swift tells us elsewhere that when Halifax, on leaving office, recommended Congreve to the generous offices of the Tories, Harley responded with a Virgilian couplet:—

> Non obtusa adeo gestamus pectora Pœni,
> Nec tam aversus equos Tyria sol jungit ab urbi.

According to Swift the Tories always treated Congreve well. There was no author of the age whose political views were less emphatic, or who less belonged to a party than Congreve. The "unreproachful man," as Gay called him, would nevertheless remember that he owed his post to Halifax, and tremble. Swift, in the verses on Dr. Delany, seems to charge Congreve with pretending to be zealous in politics to save his bread. Let us hope that it was not so, nor be too censorious if it was. England could surely spare a sinecure or two to the author of *The Way of the World.* Swift's assiduites on behalf of his Whig literary friends illustrate one of the most charming and sympathetic traits in his character.

Congreve's health grew worse and worse. On the 5th of January, 1712, Swift finds him in his lodgings almost blind, and a French physician tampering with one of his eyes. In the spring there was a change in his office, of which he vaguely speaks to Keally, and he gave up those lodgings in Arundel Street in which he had lived so long, to go into a better house in Surrey Street. During the last year there is nothing about Congreve in the *Journal to Stella,* and early in the summer of 1713 that priceless compendium of gossip comes to an end. From this time forth Congreve became more and more shadowy, and the events of the last fifteen years of his life can be very briefly recorded. In November, 1714, he ceased to be one of the Commissioners of Wine Licences, but on the 14th of that month he received a more lucrative post, that of one of the Searchers of Customs. To this was added, on the 17th of December following, the appointment of Secretary of Jamaica, and Congreve was now a rich man, the salaries of these offices amounting, it is said, to £1,200 a year. In May of the next year his old friend and patron Halifax died.

In 1717, Congreve dedicated the duodecimo edition of Dryden's *Plays* to Thomas Pelham, Duke of Newcastle, a handsome if perhaps a somewhat tardy payment of his debt of affection to the great poet who had loved him so generously in his youth. His own condition is reflected in 1719 in the Duke of Buckingham's (Mulgrave's) *Election of a Poet Laureate*, where we read:—

> Lame Congreve, unable such things to endure,
> Of Apollo begged either a crown or a cure;
> To refuse such a writer, Apollo was loath,
> And almost inclined to have given him both.

It was in this year that Congreve gave to Giles Jacob, the gossipy lawyer, those brief notes about his own life which appear in Jacob's *Poetical Register* of 1719 and 1720, and which have formed the nucleus of all succeeding biographies of Congreve. It is much to be wished that these had been fuller, or that Giles Jacob, who lived until 1744, had given us a completer version after Congreve's death. But although the poet was already regarded as a classic, and even as manifestly the leading man of letters in England, his personal life and manner seem to have excited no curiosity whatever.

Early in 1720, Dennis, now hopelessly embroiled with most of the writers of the day, assures us that he still enjoys Congreve's friendship, and on the 25th of March of the same year Pope paid the invalided dramatist the splendid compliment of dedicating his *Iliad* to him. "Instead," said the young Apollo of the new school, "of endeavouring to raise a vain monument to myself, let me leave behind me a memorial of my friendship with one of the most valuable men, as well as finest writers, of my age and country, one who has tried, and knows by experience, how hard an undertaking it is to do justice to Homer, and one who, I am sure, sincerely rejoices with me at the period of my labours." Pope showed his tact, perhaps, by selecting as the recipient of this extraordinary compliment one who was identified less than any other prominent person in England with political faction. But it is not needful to exaggerate this cleverness; there is no doubt that Pope, to whom real literary excellence was always interesting, enjoyed this opportunity of giving to a poet of an elder generation what any duke or minister in the land would have been eager to accept.

A curious note from Pope to Dennis, dated May 3rd, 1721, shows that Congreve laboured to bring these two antagonists into friendly relations, Dennis having suggested Mr. Congreve's lodgings as a suitable meeting-place for Pope and himself. On the 11th of September, Pope, writing to Gay, bids him "put Mr. Congreve in mind that he has one on this side of the world who loves him, and that there are more men and women in the universe than Mr. Gay and my Lady Duchess. There are ladies in and about Richmond who pretend to value him." All the glimpses we get of Congreve, for the future, are taken from the correspondence of his friends, among whom we may enumerate all the principal wits of the age of Anne. On the 3rd of February, 1723, Gay wrote as follows to Swift:—

Mr. Congreve I see often. He always mentions you with the strongest expressions of esteem and friendship. He labours still under the same afflictions as to his sight and gout; but, in his intervals of health, he has not lost anything of his cheerful temper. I passed all last season with him at the Bath, and I have great reason to value myself upon his friendship, for I am sure he sincerely wishes me well. We pleased ourselves with the thoughts of seeing you there.

On the 23rd of September of the same year, Swift says, in writing to Pope :—

> You must remember me with great affection to Dr. Arbuthnot, Mr. Congreve, and Gay. I think there are no more *eodem tertios* between you and me, except Mr. Jervas [the portrait painter].

About this time the friends write anxiously to one another for news of Congreve, whose constitution was now beginning to sink under these repeated attacks of the gout. On the 26th of February, 1725, he made his will, leaving the bulk of his property to Henrietta, Duchess of Marlborough, within whose influence he was now completely captivated. To the scandal of posterity, he left only £200 to Mrs. Bracegirdle, a proof, it is certain, that her former ascendency over him was now at an end. Just as Pope, Newton, and Swift exercised the gossip of their contemporaries and successors by legends of their secret nuptials, so it did not fail to be whispered that Congreve had married Mrs. Bracegirdle. That such was the fact is highly improbable. This will of 1725 contains various bequests which, in a subsequent codicil during his last illness, Congreve cancelled, mainly, it would seem, to swell the needless additions to the fortune of the Duchess.

Not Mrs. Blimber merely, but every lover of letters might wish to have been admitted, behind a curtain, to the dinner of five at Twickenham, on the 7th of July, 1726, when Pope entertained Congreve, Bolingbroke,

Gay, and Swift. About this time the inseparable companionship of Congreve and the Duchess became matter of universal comment. Pope writes in the autumn, "Mr. Congreve is too sick to brave a thin air, and she that leads him too rich to enjoy anything." On the 20th of September, 1726, Arbuthnot says that he has spent three weeks at the house of the Duchess of Marlborough, attending on Congreve, who has been like to die with a fever and the gout in his stomach, but is now convalescent again. During this dangerous illness he was well attended by his friends; Swift was constantly solicitous, and Pope went down to Windsor Park every other day to visit him. A year later, we find Swift writing to Pope:—

> Pray God continue and increase Mr. Congreve's amendment, though he does not deserve it like you, having been too lavish of that health which nature gave him.

By a not unprecedented phenomenon, just as the long-smouldering ashes of Congreve's poetry were about to be finally extinguished, a flame shot up from them. According to the anonymous author of the pamphlet, *Cobham and Congreve*, published in 1730, the *Epistle to Lord Cobham* was written shortly before Congreve died. Sir Richard Temple, for that was Lord Cobham's name before he was ennobled, had been one of the poet's dearest friends from his earliest youth. An epistle "Of Pleasing," which Congreve addressed him about 1700, speaks to him even then,

> As to one perfect in the pleasing art,
> If art it may be called in you, who seem
> By nature formed for love and for esteem,

He was for nearly thirty years the most constant of Congreve's male companions, and the most beloved of his friends. To him, then, probably in 1728, Congreve addressed the "Epistle of Improving the Present Time," perhaps the most graceful and the most happily turned of all his occasional pieces. He calls Cobham the "sincerest critic of my prose and rhyme;" and the reader of Pope's *Moral Essays* will remember how exquisite was the taste and how full the experience of this charming friend of poets. The epistle, which with its Pagan optimism troubled and irritated Swift even while he could not but praise its poetry, closes with this personal appeal:—

> Come see thy friend, retired without regret,
> Forgetting care, or striving to forget,
> In easy contemplation soothing time,
> With morals much, and now and then with rhyme;
> Not so robust in body as in mind,
> And always undejected, tho' declined;
> Not wondering at the world's new wicked ways,
> Compared with those of our forefathers' days,
> For virtue now is neither more nor less,
> And vice is only varied in the dress.
> Believe it, men have ever been the same,
> And Ovid's Golden Age is but a dream.

This equable fragment of Congreve's philosophy was printed by Curll in 1729, as soon as possible after the poet's death.

The end was now approaching. In the early spring of 1728, Congreve went down to Bath with Gay and the Duchess of Marlborough, and during the summer and autumn, Gay, who remained at Bath, sends bulletins and messages from Congreve to Pope and Swift. It was on his return from this long visit to Bath, in the autumn of 1728, that Congreve's coach was upset, and he, in his helpless condition, severely injured. He did not succumb at once to this accident, but continuing to complain of a pain in his side, gradually grew weaker, and passed away in his house in Surrey Street, Strand, at five o'clock on Sunday morning, the 19th of January, 1729, wanting three weeks of the completion of his fifty-ninth year. On the following Sunday, between nine and ten in the evening, after his body had lain in state in Jerusalem Chamber, it was carried with great pomp into King Henry the Seventh's chapel, and then, after the funeral service was over, was buried in the Abbey. The pall was carried by the Duke of Bridgewater, the Earl of Godolphin (who represented his wife, the Duchess of Marlborough), Lord Cobham, and Lord Wilmington.

It is understood that the Duchess of Marlborough profited from the loss of her witty and easy-going friend to the amount of £10,000. She was in no want of money; she had already more than she could waste, but she deserves a mild sort of credit for spending some of Congreve's bequest in his honour. She placed in Westminster Abbey the marble tablet on which may still be read the inscription which follows:—

Mr. William Congreve died Jan. the 19th, 1728 [old style], aged fifty-six [*sic*], and was buried near this place; to whose most valuable memory this monument is set up by Henrietta, Duchess of Marlborough, as a mark how deeply she remembers the happiness and honour she enjoyed in the sincere friendship of so worthy and honest a man, whose virtue, candour, and wit gained him the love and esteem of the present age, and whose writings will be the admiration of the future.

Her mother, the old Duchess, the formidable Sarah, came to read this epitaph, and turning away made a cruel misquotation,—"I know not what 'pleasure' she might have had in his company, but I am sure it was no 'honour.'" It seems that the young Duchess was almost crazy in her devotion to the poet's memory. She had a figure made, according to one account an ivory automaton, according to others a waxen statue, life-size, and exactly like him, which sat in Congreve's clothes at her table, and was so contrived as to nod mechanically when she spoke to it. Her *ennui* went to such lengths that she had the feet of this figure wrapped in cloths, as poor Congreve's gouty feet had been, while a physician attended on the statue, and pretended to diagnose its daily condition. The Duchess showed Young, the poet, a diamond necklace, on which she spent seven thousand pounds, all that remained of Congreve's bequest after she had indulged in these Tussaud-like vagaries. Well might the author of the *Night Thoughts* exclaim, "How much better would it have been for Congreve to have given the money to poor Mrs. Bracegirdle!" Leigh Hunt somewhat cynically suggested that the legacy to the Duchess was intended to pay for all the dinners he had eaten and the wine he had drunk at her expense.

Congreve was deeply regretted by wiser friends than Henrietta, Duchess of Marlborough. On the 13th of February, 1729, Swift summed up the position in his wholesome and incisive way :—

This renews the grief for the death of our friend Mr. Congreve, whom I loved from my youth, and who, surely, beside his other talents, was a very agreeable companion. He had the misfortune to squander away a very good constitution in his younger days ; and I think a man of sense and merit like him is bound in conscience to preserve his health for the sake of his friends, as well as of himself. Upon his own account I could not much desire the continuance of his life, under so much pain and so many infirmities. Years have not yet hardened me, and I have an addition of weight on my spirits since we lost him, though I saw him seldom, and possibly, if he had lived on, should never have seen him more.

Mrs. Whiteway, long afterwards, told Lord Orrery that letters from Congreve to Swift still existed; these seem to have disappeared, and so have the letters, possibly with gossip about literature and London in them, with which Congreve is known to have beguiled the exile of Lady Mary Wortley Montagu. Of the poetical associates of his youth, Southerne alone outlived him, for Vanbrugh had died in 1726.

CHAPTER V.

IT is not very easy to construct a definite portrait of Congreve. He was a handsome, plump man, whom Sir Godfrey Kneller painted for the Kit-Cat Club in a velvet coat and in that voluminous fair periwig which delighted Thackeray so much. He looks at us with his fine dark eyes, and he points with bediamonded forefinger towards the beauties of a sylvan scene; but the picture scarcely gives us an indication of what this elegant personage may have been at his ease, and among his intimates. Yet it is certain that it was at the chimney-corner that he showed off to most advantage, commonly in the evening, and after a repast washed down by profuse and genial wines. He was eminently good-natured, "unreproachful" as Gay called him. No unkind word is recorded of Congreve in all the bitter gossip of two generations. The only moderately unkind thing he is ever reported to have done is told us by a witness whom we need not believe. When Lady Mary Montagu said that Congreve laughed at Pope's verses, she was herself too angry with Pope to be a candid witness. Every one liked Congreve, he had sympathy, urbanity, witty talk, a gentlemanly acquiescence, an ear at everybody's service, while Steele might follow Swift, Dennis succeed Pope, at Congreve's lodgings without a momentary sense of embarrassment or ill-temper.

But when we have said this we have said almost all we know. There were no salient points about Congreve's character. Though an old bachelor, he was not eccentric; though a man of pleasure, he was discreet. No vagaries, no escapades, place him in a ludicrous or in a human light. He passes through the literary life of his time as if in felt slippers, noiseless, unupbraiding, without personal adventures. Even the too-picturesque Mrs. Delarivière Manley can make nothing of his smiling, faultless rotundity. It is evident, I think, that in this hitherto unnoticed page of her *New Atalantis* she is endeavouring to draw Congreve and Mrs. Bracegirdle:—

> Be pleased to direct your eyes towards the pair of beaux in the next chariot. . . . He on the right is a near favourite of the Muses; he has touched the drama with truer art than any of his contemporaries, comes nearer nature and the ancients, unless in his last performance, which indeed met with most applause, however least deserving. But he seemed to know what he did, descending from himself to write to the Many, whereas before he wrote to the Few. I find a wonderful deal of good sense in that gentleman; he has wit, without the pride and affectation that generally accompanies, and always corrupts it.
>
> His Myra is as celebrated as Ovid's Corinna, and as well-known. How happy is he in the favour of that lovely lady! She, too, deserves applause, besides her beauty, for her gratitude and sensibility to so deserving an admirer. There are few women, who, when they once give in to the sweets of an irregular passion, care to confine themselves to him that first endeared it to them, but not so the charming Myra.

Anthony Aston, who calls Mrs. Bracegirdle, "the

Diana of the stage," thought that even to Congreve she was no more than a friend. But he tells us that she was very fond of the poet, and was always uneasy at his leaving her, especially as his presence at her side protected her from the importunities of such fiery lovers as Lord Lovelace. There is no doubt she was a very pure-minded and a very amiable woman, so charitable that the poor of Clare Market were ready to form a bodyguard to shield her from the impertinence of the beaux.

Of Congreve's wit in conversation there is no question. We have seen what Swift thought of it, and Lady Mary, who had had opportunities of judging, told Spence that she never knew anybody that had so much wit as Congreve. He was one of the celebrated coterie of thirty-nine men of genius and quality, who met in Shire Lane to eat Christopher Katt's mutton-pies, and who became the Kit-Cat Club. From its rise in 1700 to its close about 1710, Congreve was the life of this brilliant gathering. But we possess no record of his colloquial powers; a joke about Gay's voracity is passably funny, but not enough to build a reputation on. We shall not laugh at Congreve's repartees till we can tell what songs the Sirens sang, and we must take the reputation of his good fellowship upon faith. Pope and Tonson agreed that Garth, Vanbrugh, and Congreve were "the three most honest-hearted real good men of the poetical members" of the Club.

One thing which Congreve said, apparently in all seriousness, has become more famous than any example of his wit, and may probably be known to thousands of persons who never read a line of his writings. This is his remark to Voltaire when that eminent Frenchman went to call upon him. It may be well to quote the whole passage from Voltaire's *Letters concerning the English Nation*:—

Mr. Congreve raised the glory of comedy to a greater height than any English writer before or since his time. He wrote only a few plays, but they are excellent in their kind. The laws of the drama are strictly observed in them. They abound with characters, all which are shadowed with the utmost delicacy, and we don't meet with so much as one low or coarse jest. The language is everywhere that of men of fashion, but their actions are those of knaves, a proof that he was perfectly well acquainted with human nature, and frequented what we call polite company.

He was infirm, and come to the verge of life when I knew him. Mr. Congreve had one defect, which was his entertaining too mean an idea of his own first profession, that of a writer, though it was to this he owed his fame and fortune. He spoke of his works as trifles that were beneath him, and hinted to me in our first conversation, that I should visit him upon no other foot than that of a gentleman who led a life of plainness and simplicity. I answered that had he been so unfortunate as to be a mere gentleman, I should never have come to see him; and I was very much disgusted at so unseasonable a piece of vanity.

The anecdote is interesting and valuable, but perhaps we need not be so much disgusted at Congreve's attitude as Voltaire was. We must remember that the incident occurred in 1726, very late in Congreve's life, when literary ambition, and, above all, the charming pleasure of easy composition, had long abandoned him. May not what Voltaire took to be vanity have been really modesty? May not the aged and "unreproachful" poet, separated from his own writings by so many sterile years, have come to think his original gifts mediocre, and have been genuinely a little embarrassed at Voltaire's effusive flattery? A young poet with all the world to conquer, and with the rhymes automatically carolling at the tip of his tongue, can scarcely conceive the indifference, the chagrin, of an aged man of letters, stricken with silence, with never a drop of ichor left in his shrunken vein. I think that the world has judged Congreve very absurdly in so easily accepting Voltaire's account of this interview. The poet can scarcely have been such a snob as Voltaire indicates; if he had entertained a mean idea of the literary profession, we should have heard of it from Swift or Pope. Weary and disappointed, left behind in the race of life by nimbler wits, tortured by that dreadful sterility that had stricken him at thirty, it is probable that Voltaire's voluble literary compliments seemed to Congreve to present an element of possible banter. It was safer, in that case, to pose as "a gentleman who led a life of plainness and simplicity," than as the Apollo of the drama. It was prudence in a gouty old person of quality to avoid being led too far afield by this brilliant and inquisitive Frenchman. It is an odd example of the fate that attends man's words, that this solitary example of reserve has prejudiced Congreve with myriads of readers who would otherwise have no dislike to his character.

In one of his letters to Keally, Congreve says, "You know me enough to know that I feel very sensibly and silently for those whom I love." This word "silently" seems to express him very well. He made no protestations, he was never a *poseur*; but all through life his friends seem to have known that they could depend upon him. His tastes extended a little way ahead of his age. He had a small collection of pictures.[1] In June, 1703, he paid Kneller £45 for a St. Cecilia, a very large price for an English painting in those days. Oldys tells us that he collected chap-books and old ballads, a whim which even the antiquary seems to think would seem "diverting to a satirical genius." It may be mentioned that during part of his life, at all events, Congreve possessed a little country house at Northall, a village three miles north-east of Ivinghoe, in Bucks. When he went there first he must have been still in his athletic youth, for he speaks of "jumping one-and-twenty feet at one jump on Northall Common." This sounds a good record for a poet "more fat than bard beseems."

The reputation of Congreve has undergone many reverses, but will probably never again sink so far as it

[1] This note, without post-mark, addressed to Mr. Porter, is among the British Museum letters (Add. MSS. 4293):—

SR.

if you see Mr. Custis to night pray know of him if it be possible for me to have a picture of Ld. Rochester which was Mrs. Barrys. I think it is a head. I think it is not as a painting any very great matter. however I have a very particular reason why I woud have it at any reasonable rate, at least the refusal of it. if this can de don. he will very much oblige his &

yr.
very humble Servant
WM CONGREVE.

fryday even :

did half a century ago. In the early Victorian age, his plays almost ceased to be praised, and perhaps to be read, while every humanitarian passerby thought it easy to cast his stone of reproach at these "artificial," "heartless," and "immoral" comedies. Of late years the fame of our greatest comic playwright has been eloquently defended, and it is doubtful whether any critic of responsibility would, at the present day, be found to endorse the old strain of condemnation by the moral test. Charles Lamb, extreme and paradoxical as his famous essay on "Artificial Comedy" may have been, did infinite good in distinguishing the temper in which works of amusement and those of edification should be considered, and in defending the easy-going dramatists of the seventeenth century from the charge of being injurious to society.

There is much to be said for Lamb's theory that the stage of Congreve and Vanbrugh was never intended to represent real life, but merely created in order to form a "sanctuary and quiet Alsatia," where the mind could take refuge for a while when hunted by the casuistries of Puritanism. But the weak points of this argument are easily divined, and what is really valuable in Lamb's vindication is the appeal to another tribunal than the court where the Young Person sits enthroned, a Rhadamanthus of the minor morals. The result of Lamb's eloquent special pleading has been to make English critics feel that when it is said that Congreve is not "proper," the last word has not been spoken, and that though his standard of decency is not our own, nor ever likely to be resumed, his merits as an artist are not on that account to be overlooked or underrated. In this connection, and bearing in mind the fluctuations of sentiment upon this question of propriety, we may recollect that Voltaire, in a passage quoted above, gives special praise to Congreve for the purity of his language. Decency of expression is mainly a conventional or comparative matter. In the seventeenth century divines said things to their congregations, and sons wrote anecdotes to their mothers, which to-day would sound crude in the smoking-room of a club, and it was rather Congreve's misfortune than his fault that he happened to flourish as a writer, at the very moment when, in all their history, Englishmen and Englishwomen were allowing themselves the broadest license in expression, and the freest examination of scabrous situations. To dwell any further on this much-discussed difficulty in this place seems needless. It is enough to warn the lamb-like reader, if there be such an one, that in the menagerie of the Restoration dramatists he must expect to find lions.

The position of Congreve in the brief and splendid series of our comic playwrights is easily defined. Etheredge led the van with his French inspiration, directly drawn from Molière, his delicate observation, his lightness of touch, his thin elegance. Wycherley followed with his superior strength, his massive dialogue, his pungent wit, his vigour, his invention. There could be no finer introduction to the art of comedy than was suggested by the experiments of these two playwrights. But they were merely transitional figures, they pointed the way to a greater master. Looked at as a final expression of a national art, the work of Etheredge would have seemed flimsy in its lightness, weak in its delicacy, while that of Wycherley was rough, hard, and unfinished. The natural complement of these two writers was a poet who should combine their excellencies, be fine and yet strong, patient to finish as well as spirited to sketch. It was when the public had grown familiar with the types of writing exemplified at their best in *The Man of Mode* and *The Plain Dealer*, that Congreve came forward with his erudite and brilliant comedies, combining the quality of Etheredge with that of Wycherley, adding much from Molière, owing much to his own trained and active fancy, and placing English comedy of manners for the first time on a really classic basis. By the side of the vivid characters in *Love for Love*, the group that dances round Sir Fopling Flutter seems a cloud of phantoms, and the Horners and Manleys no better than violent caricatures of humanity.

With all his genius, with all his opportunity of position, Congreve did not reach the highest level. The perfection of which we have been speaking is relative, and in comparison with Molière, the English comedian takes a second rank in all but wit. It is remarkable that while in most branches of literature the English have excelled in preserving the spirit of great writing while treating the forms and recognized types very cavalierly, in this one matter of the Comedy of Manners they failed to take the highest place precisely through their timid adherence to the rules of composition. If Congreve could have been forced out into a wider life, persuaded to disregard the restrictions of artificial comedy, obliged to draw men where and as he observed them, if, in other words, he could have written in a more English fashion, there is no apparent reason why he might not now stand close by the shoulder of Molière. The Englishmen who immediately followed him, Vanbrugh and Farquhar, with much less art than he, and genius decidedly inferior, have put themselves sometimes almost on a level with Congreve through their very audacity, their disregard of rules. Not one of their comedies, if carefully analyzed, reveals the science, the balance of parts, the delicate literary skill of Congreve, but their scenes are apt to be so much breezier than his, their characters have so much more blood and bustle, that we over-estimate their relative value in comparison with Congreve. Yet, with all his limitations, he remains the principal figure in English comedy of manners, one of the secondary glories of our language and literature, and in his own narrow kind unsurpassed even by such broader and more genial masters as Terence and Molière.

On one side the excellence of Congreve seems unique among the comic dramatists of the world. He is probably, of them all, the one whose plays are written with the most unflagging wit and literary charm. The style of Congreve lifts him high above all his English rivals, and there is no test so unfair to Wycherley or to Farquhar as that of comparing a fragment of their work with an analogous fragment of his. Hazlitt has excellently said that Congreve's comedies "are a singular treat to those who have cultivated a taste for the niceties of English style: there is a peculiar flavour in the very words, which is to be found in hardly any other writer." What we call his wit, that which makes his scenes so uniformly dazzling, consists, in a great measure, in this inexplicable felicity of phrase, this invariable selection of the unexpected and yet obviously the best word. In this art of diction he resembles none of his own sturdy contemporaries; the sentences are as limpid as Addison's, as melodious as Berkeley's, as highly coloured as Sterne's, and this quality of his style makes Congreve very interesting to the student. He stands on the threshold of the eighteenth century, and seems to have an intuition of all its peculiar graces.

Yet every admirer of Congreve has experienced the fatigue that this very brilliance, this unflagging glitter of style produces. It is altogether beyond not credibility only, but patience. The prodigality of wit becomes wearisome, and at last only emphasizes the absence of tenderness, simplicity, and genuine imagination. It is at such a moment that Thackeray steps in, and throwing the shutters suddenly open, floods the stage of Congreve with the real light of life, and in a few marvellous pages disenchants us of his "tawdry play-house taper." But we must not permit the intrusion. There is a sunshine that filters through the dewy hawthorn-branches, there is a wax-light that flashes back from the sconces of an alcove, but these are not compatible, and the latter is not justly to be extinguished by the former. In the comedies of Congreve we breathe an atmosphere of the most exquisite artificial refinement, an air of literary frangipan or millefleur-water. What we have to admire in them is the polish, the grace, the extreme technical finish, the spectacle of an intellect of rare cultivation and power concentrating itself on the creation of a microcosm swarming with human volvox and vibrion. If we are prepared to accept this, and to ask no more than this from Congreve, we shall not grudge him his permanent station among the great writers of this country.

THE END.

APPENDIX.

THE notes supplied by Southerne exist, in the handwriting of that poet, in the British Museum. As they have never been printed in their original form, I have thought it interesting to transcribe them verbatim. The press-mark is Add. MSS. 4221 :—

Mr. Will. Congreve was the Son of a younger brother of a good old family in Staffordshire, who was employd in the stewardship of part of the great estate of ye Earl of Burlington in Ireland, where he resided many years, his only son the Poet was born in that Country, went to the free school at Kilkenny, and from thence to Trinity College in Dublin, where he had the advantage of being educated under a polite schollar, and ingenious Gentleman Dr. St. George Ash, who was after Provost of that College, then Bp. of Cloghar, and then Bp. of Derry. this Bp. had the great good fortune of haveing the two famusest Witts his pupills the most extraordinary Dr. Swift, Dean of St. Patricks, and Mr. Will. Congreve, tho not at the same time. Mr. Congreve was of the Middle Temple, his first performance was an ~~ingenious~~ Novel, calld incognita, then he began his Play the old Batchelor haveing little Acquaintance withe the traders in that way, his Cozens recommended him to a friend of theirs,[1] who was very usefull to him in the whole course of his

[1] Probably Southerne himself.

play, he engag'd Mr. Dryden in its favour, who upon reading it sayd he never saw such a first play in his life, but the Author not being acquainted with the stage or the town, it would be pity to have it miscarry for want of a little Assistance : the stuff was rich indeed, it wanted only the fashionable cutt of the town. To help that Mr. Dryden, Mr. Manwayring, and Mr. Southern red it with great care, and Mr. Dryden putt it in the order it was playd, Mr. Southerne obtaind of Mr. Thos : Davenant who then governd the Playhouse, that Mr. Congreve shoud have the privilege of the Playhouse half a year before his play was playd, wh. I never knew allowd any one before : it was playd with great success that play made him many friends, Mr. Montacue, after Ld. Hallyfax was his Patron, putt him into the Commission for hackney coaches, and then into the Pipe Office, and then gave him a Patent place in the Customs of 600 Pds. per ann. and Secretary to Jamaica, yt payd him 700 Pounds a year by deputy on ye Exchange at Lond.

This document is endorsed, probably in the hand of John Campbell, "Memoirs relating to Mr. Congreve written by Mr. Thomas Southern, and communicated to me from him by the hands of Dr. Thomas Pellett, January 12th, $173\frac{5}{6}$." Southerne died so late as May 26, 1746, at the age of eighty-seven.

INDEX.

D.

E.

F.

G.

H.

I.

J.

BIBLIOGRAPHY.

BY

JOHN P. ANDERSON

(British Museum).

I. WORKS.
II. DRAMATIC WORKS.
III. POEMS.
IV. SINGLE WORKS.
V. MISCELLANEOUS.
VI. APPENDIX—
  Biography, Criticism, etc.
  Magazine Articles.
VII. CHRONOLOGICAL LIST OF WORKS.

I. WORKS.

The First (— Third) Volume of the Works of Mr. William Congreve. 3 vols. London, 1710, 8vo.

The pagination is continuous throughout, and the several pieces have distinct title-pages. There is another issue of this edition, with a collective title-page bearing date 1717.

——The Works of Mr. William Congreve. Third edition, revised by the author. London, 1719-20, 12mo.

The several pieces have separate title-pages.

——Fifth edition. 3 vols. London, 1730, 12mo.

——Another edition. 3 vols. London, 1753, 12mo.

——Another edition. 3 vols. Birmingham, 1761, 8vo.

——Another edition. 3 vols. Dublin, 1773, 16mo.

——Seventh edition. To which is prefixed the life of the author. 2 vols. London, 1774, 12mo.

II. DRAMATIC WORKS.

The Dramatic Works of William Congreve. Containing The Old Bachelor; The Way of the World; Love for Love; The Mourning Bride; The Double

Dealer. 5 pts. Dublin, 1731, 12mo.

Each play has a separate title-page and pagination; Nos. 2 and 3 were published in 1730 and 1729 respectively.

The Dramatic Works of William Congreve. (Concerning humour in comedy. A letter—Amendments of Mr. Collier's citations from the Old Bachelor, etc.) 2 vols. London, 1773, 12mo.

The Dramatic Works of Wycherley, Congreve, Vanbrugh, and Farquhar. With biographical and critical notices by Leigh Hunt. London, 1849, 8vo.

The Best Plays of the Old Dramatists. William Congreve. Edited by Alexander Charles Ewald. London, 1887, 8vo.

III. POEMS.

The Poetical Works of Will. Congreve. (*Bell's Edition. The Poets of Great Britain*, vol. lxvi.) Edinburg, 1778, 12mo.

The Poems of Congreve and Fenton. (*Works of the English Poets, by Samuel Johnson*, vol. xxix.) London, 1779, 8vo.

Another edition. (*Works of the English Poets, by Samuel Johnson*, vol. xxxiv.) London, 1790, 8vo.

The Poetical Works of William Congreve. (*Anderson's Poets of Great Britain*, vol. vii.) Edinburgh, 1793, 8vo.

Select Poems of William Congreve. (*Park's Works of the British Poets, Supplement, etc.*) London, 1809, 16mo.

The Poems of William Congreve. (*Chalmers' Works of the English Poets*, vol. x.) London, 1810, 8vo.

Select Poems of William Congreve, with a life of the Author. (*Sandford's Works of the British Poets*, vol. xiv.) Philadelphia, 1819, 12mo.

IV. SINGLE WORKS.

Amendments upon Mr. Collier's false and imperfect citations [in his "Short View of the Profaneness, etc., of the English Stage"] from the Old Batchelour, Double Dealer, Love for Love, Mourning Bride. By the author of those plays. London, 1698, 8vo.

The Birth of the Muse: a poem. London, 1698, fol.

The Double Dealer: a comedy. [In five acts and in prose.] London, 1694, 4to.

——Another edition. London [1694 ?], 8vo.

——Another edition. [London], 1711, 8vo.

——Another edition. (*Collection of English Plays*, vol. vii.) London [1711], 8vo.

——Another edition. London, 1735, 12mo.

——Another edition. London, 1739, 12mo.

——Another edition. (*Bell's British Theatre*, vol. xiii.) London, 1777, 12mo.

——Another edition. (*New English Theatre*, vol. ix.) London, 1777, 8vo.

——Another edition. (*Bell's British Theatre*, vol. xxviii.) London, 1797, 8vo.

——Another edition, revised by J. P. Kemble. London [1802], 8vo.

The Double Dealer. Another edition. (*Modern British Drama*, vol. iii.) London, 1811, 8vo.
——Another edition. Revised by J. P. Kemble, etc. London, 1815, 8vo.
——Another edition. (*Dibdin's London Theatre*, vol. xx.) London, 1816, 16mo.
——Another edition. (*London Stage*, vol. iv.) London [1824], 8vo.
——Another edition. (*Acting Drama.*) London, 1834, 8vo.
Incognita: or, Love and Duty reconçil'd. By Cleophil. London, 1692, 8vo.
——Another edition. London, 1700, 8vo.
——Another edition. London, 1713, 8vo.
——Another edition. London, 1713, 12mo.
The Judgment of Paris: a Masque. London, 1701, 4to.
——Another edition. [London, 1778 ?], 8vo.
A letter [in verse] to Viscount Cobham [on various subjects]. London, 1729, fol.
Love for Love. A comedy. [In five acts and in prose.] London, 1695, 4to.
——Second edition. London, 1695, 4to.
——Another edition. London [1695 ?], 8vo.
——Another edition. (*Collection of English Plays*, vol. vii.] London, 1720, 8vo.
——Another edition. London, 1720, 8vo.
——Another edition. London, 1733, 12mo.
——Another edition. London, 1747, 12mo.
——Another edition. (*Bell's British Theatre*, vol. viii.) London, 1776, 12mo.
——Another edition. (*New English Theatre*, vol. v.) London, 1776, 8vo.
——Another edition. (*Bell's British Theatre*, vol. i.) London, 1797, 8vo.
——Another edition. (*Inchbald's British Theatre*, vol. xiii.) London, 1808, 12mo.
——Another edition. (*Modern British Drama*, vol. iii., *Comedies.*) London, 1811, 8vo.
——Another edition. (*Dibdin's London Theatre*, vol. xvi.) London, 1815, 16mo.
——Another edition. (*London Stage*, vol. iii.) London [1824], 8vo.
——Another edition. (*British Drama*, vol. ii.) London, 1826, 8vo.
——Another edition. (*Cumberland's British Theatre*, vol. xix.) London [1829 ?], 12mo.
——Another edition. (*Acting Drama.*) London, 1834, 8vo.
——Another edition. (*British Drama*, vol. x.) London, 1872, 8vo.
—— ——Congreve's Comedy of Love for Love revised, curtailed, and altered by J. W. Wallack. Marked, as acted, by H. B. Phillips. New York, 1854, 12mo.
—— ——Buxom Joan of Lymas [*i.e.*, Limehouse]'s Love to a Jolly Sailor; or the Maiden's Choice; being Love for Love again, etc. [The first three verses taken from W. Congreve's Love for Love. With the musical notes. London [1695 ?], s. sh. fol.
The Mourning Bride. A tragedy.

[In five acts, and in verse.] London, 1697, 4to.
——Second edition. London, 1679 [1697], 4to.
——Second edition. London, 1697, 12mo.
——Another edition. London [1697 ?], 8vo.
——Another edition. (*Collection of English Plays*, vol. viii.) London [1711], 8vo.
——Another edition. London, 1776, 8vo.
——Another edition. (*New English Theatre*, vol. iv.) London, 1776, 8vo.
——Another edition. (*Bell's British Theatre*, vol. iii.) London, 1776, 12mo.
——Another edition. London, 1777, 8vo.
——Another edition. (*Bell's British Theatre*, vol. xix.) London, 1797, 8vo.
——Another edition. (*Inchbald's British Theatre*, vol. xiii.) London, 1808, 12mo.
——Another edition. (*Modern British Drama*, vol. i.) London, 1811, 8vo.
——Another edition. (*Dibdin's London Theatre*, vol. xi.) London, 1815, 16mo.
——Another edition. Edinburgh [1820 ?], 12mo.
——Another edition. (*British Drama*, vol. i.) London, 1824, 8vo.
——Another edition. (*London Stage*, vol. iv.) London [1824], 8vo.
——Another edition. (*British Drama*, vol. iii.) London, 1865, 8vo.

The Mourning Muse of Alexis. A pastoral lamenting the death of Queen Mary, etc. London, 1695, fol.
——Second edition. London, 1695, fol.
——Third edition. Dublin, 1695, fol.
——Another edition. (*Collection of English Poetry*, vol. ii.) London, 1709, 8vo.

The Old Bachelor. A Comedy [in five acts and in prose]. London, 1693, 4to.
——Second edition. London, 1693, 4to.
——Another edition. London, [1693], 8vo.
——Sixth edition, corrected. London, 1697, 4to.
——Another edition. London, 1710, 8vo.
——Another edition. (*Collection of English Plays*, vol. vii.) London, 1720, 8vo.
——Another edition. (*Bell's British Theatre*, vol. ii.) London, 1776, 12mo.
——Another edition. (*New English Theatre*, vol. iii.) London, 1776, 8vo.
——Another edition. London, 1781, 8vo.
——Another edition. (*Bell's British Theatre*, vol. xxviii.) London, 1797, 8vo.
——Another edition. (*Modern British Drama*, vol. iii.) London, 1811, 8vo.

A Pindarique Ode, humbly offer'd to the King on his taking Namure. London, 1695, fol.

A Pindarique Ode, humbly offer'd to the Queen on the victorious progress of Her Majesty's arms, under the conduct of the Duke of Marlborough. To which is prefixed a discourse on the

Pindarique Ode. London, 1706, fol.
The Story of Semele. [An opera, in three parts and in verse.] Altered from the Semele of William Congreve, set to musick by Mr. G. F. Handel. London, 1744, 4to.
The words only. Semele first appeared in the "Works," 1710.
——Semele [an oratorio in three parts]. Alter'd from the Semele of Congreve. London, 1762, 4to.
The Tears of Amaryllis for Amyntas; a pastoral on the death of the Marquis of Blandford, etc. London, 1705, fol.
The Way of the World. A Comedy. [In five acts, and in prose.] London, 1700, 4to.
——Another edition. London [1700 ?], 12mo.
——Second edition. London, 1706, 4to.
——Another edition. (*Collection of English Plays*, vol. vii.) London [1720], 8vo.
——Another edition. London, 1735, 12mo.
——Another edition. (*New English Theatre*, vol. v.) London, 1776, 8vo.
——Another edition. (*Bell's British Theatre*, vol. xi.) London, 1777, 12mo.
Another edition. (*Bell's British Theatre*, vol. xxxiii.) London, 1797, 8vo.
——Another edition. Revised by J. P. Kemble, etc. London [1800], 8vo.
——Another edition. (*Modern British Drama*, vol. iii.) Lon- 1811, 8vo.
——Another edition. Revised by J. P. Kemble, etc. London, 1815, 8vo.
——Another edition. (*Dibdin's London Theatre*, vol. xxiv.) London, 1818, 16mo.
——Another edition. (*London Stage*, vol. iv.) London [1824], 8vo.
——Another edition. (*British Drama*, vol. xi.) London, 1872, 8vo.

V. MISCELLANEOUS.

The Dramatic Works of John Dryden. [Edited by W. Congreve.] 6 vols. London, 1717, 12mo.
——Another edition. 6 vols. London, 1735, 12mo.
——Another edition. 6 vols. London, 1762, 12mo.
Epistle [in verse] on Retirement and Taste. (*Miscellany on Taste, by Pope.*) London, 1732, 8vo.
An essay concerning humour in Comedy.
See "Letters upon several occasions."
Hymn to Venus, translated by William Congreve. (*Minor Poems of Homer.*) New York, 1872, 8vo.
Letters upon several occasions; written by and between Mr. Dryden, Mr. Wycherly, Mr. Congreve, and Mr. Dennis, etc. [Contains "An Essay concerning Humour."] London, 1696, 8vo.
——Another edition. (*Select Works of John Dennis*, vol. ii.) London, 1718, 8vo.
Mr. Congreve's Last Will and Testament; with characters of his writings by Mr. Dryden,

Sir R. Blackmore, Mr. Addison, and Major Pack. To which are added two pieces—viz., I. Of rightly improving the present time, an epistle [in verse] from Mr. Congreve. II. The Game of Quadrille, an allegory. London, 1729, 8vo.

Miscelleneous 'Works written by His Grace, late Duke of Buckingham; also State Poems on the late times by Dryden, Etheridge, Sheppard, Butler, Earl of D(orset), Congreve, etc. London, 1704, 8vo.

Ovid's Art of Love, in three books. Together with his Remedy of Love. Translated into English verse by several eminent hands [J. Dryden, W. Congreve, and N. Tate]. London, 1709, 8vo.
Numerous editions.

Ovid's Metamorphoses, in fifteen books. Translated [into English verse] by the most eminent hands [J. Dryden, J. Addison, L. Eusden, W. Congreve, etc.]. London, 1717, fol.

——Fifth edition. 2 vols. London, 1751, 12mo.

——Another edition. 2 vols. New York, 1815, 12mo.

Tales and Novels in verse. From the French of La Fontaine, by several hands [Topham, W. Congreve, and others]. Published by S. Humphreys. Edinburgh, 1762, 12mo.

Verses sacred to the Memory of Grace, Lady Gethin, etc. (*Lady Gethin's Misery is Vertues Whetstone.*) London, 1703, 4to.

Works of Juvenal and Persius, translated by John Dryden (William Congreve) and others. London, 1693, fol.

——Another edition. (*Anderson's Poets of Great Britain*, vol. xii.) London, 1793, etc., 8vo.

——Another edition. (*British Poets*, vol. xcvii.) Chiswick, 1822, 12mo.

VI. APPENDIX.

Biography, Criticism, etc.

Baker, David Erskine. — Biographia Dramatica; or, a companion to the Playhouse, etc. 3 vols. London, 1812, 8vo.
Congreve, vol. i., pp. 141-144.

Berkeley, George Monck.—Literary relics: containing original letters from King Charles II., Steele, Congreve, etc. London, 1789, 8vo.

Biographia Britannica. — Biographia Britannica: or, the lives of the most eminent persons, etc. 6 vols. London, 1747-66, fol.
William Congreve, vol. iii., pp. 1439-1449.

Cibber, Theophilus.—The Lives of the Poets of Great Britain and Ireland. By T. Cibber [R. Shiels and others]. 5 vols. London, 1753, 12mo.
William Congreve, vol. iv., pp. 83-98.

Coleridge, Hartley. — Biographia Borealis; or, lives of distinguished Northerns. London, 1833, 8vo.
William Congreve, pp. 665-693.

Congreve, William.—Animadversions on Mr. Congreve's late answer to Mr. Collier, in a dialogue. And some offers towards new-modeling the stage. London, 1698, 8vo.

——Second edition. London, 1698, 8vo.

Congreve, William.—A Letter to Mr. Congreve on his pretended amendments, etc., of Mr. Collier's Short View of the Immorality and Prophaneness of the English Stage. London, 1698, 8vo.
——The Temple of Fame; a poem, inscribed to Mr. Congreve. London, 1709, 12mo.
——A Poem to the Memory of Mr. Congreve. [By James Thomson.] London, 1729, 8vo.
——Another edition. [Edited by Rev. H. J. Cary for the Percy Society.] London, 1843, 8vo.

Crawfurd, Oswald. — English Comic Dramatists. Edited by O. Crawfurd. London, 1883, 8vo.
Congreve, pp. 129-160.

Davies, Thomas.—Dramatic Miscellanies, etc. 3 vols. London, 1784, 8vo.
Congreve, vol. iii., pp. 311-382.

Doran, J.—Annals of the English Stage, from Thomas Betterton to Edmund Kean. Edited by Robert W. Lowe. 3 vols. London, 1888, 8vo.
Numerous references to Congreve.

Dryden, John.—The Critical and Miscellaneous Prose Works of John Dryden. With an account of the Life and Writings of the author, by Edmond Malone. 3 vols. London, 1800, 8vo.
Numerous references to Congreve.

Genest, J.—Some account of the English Stage, from the Restoration in 1660 to 1830. [By J. Genest.] 10 vols. Bath, 1832, 8vo.
References to Congreve, vol. ii.

Gosse, Edmund W. — English Odes, selected by E. W. Gosse. (*Parchment Library.*) London, 1881, 8vo.
Congreve is noticed in the Introduction, and an ode "On Mrs. Arabella Hunt's Singing" is included in the collection.

Grisy, A. de.—Histoire de la Comédie Anglaise (1672-1707). Paris, 1878, 8vo.
Congreve, pp. 151-257.

Hayman, Rev. Samuel.—The New Handbook for Youghal, etc. Youghal, 1858, 8vo.
References to Congreve, pp. 53 and 55.

Hazlitt, William.—A View of the English Stage, etc. London, 1818, 8vo.
"Love for Love," pp. 226-229.
——Lectures on the English Comic Writers, etc. London, 1819, 8vo.
Wycherley, Congreve, Vanbrugh, and Farquhar, pp. 133-176.

Hunt, Leigh. — The Dramatic Works of Wycherley, Congreve, Vanbrugh, and Farquhar. London, 1849, 8vo.
Biographical and critical notice of Congreve, pp. xix.-xxxviii.

Jacob, Giles.—The Poetical Register; or, the lives and characters of the English dramatic poets, etc. 2 vols. London, 1719, 1720, 8vo.
William Congreve, vol. i., pp. 41-46; vol. ii., pp. 248-250.

Johnson, Samuel.—The lives of the most eminent English Poets, etc. 4 vols. London, 1781, 8vo.
Congreve, vol. iii., pp. 43-69.

L'Estrange, Rev. A. G.—History of English Humour, etc. 2 vols. London, 1878, 8vo.
Congreve, vol. i., pp. 355-358.

Macaulay, Thomas Babington.—Critical and Historical Essays, contributed to the *Edinburgh Review.* 3 vols. London, 1843, 8vo.
Comic Dramatists of the Restoration, vol. iii., pp. 255-312.

Moyle, Walter.—The whole works

of Walter Moyle, etc. London, 1727, 8vo.
Letters from Congreve, pp. 227 and 231.

Nichols, John.—Literary Anecdotes of the eighteenth century, etc. 9 vols. London, 1812-1815, 8vo.
Numerous references to Congreve.

Notes and Queries. General Index to Notes and Queries. Five series. London, 1856-1880, 4to.
References to William Congreve.

The Justice of Peace; or, A Vindication of Peace from several late pamphlets, written by Mr. Congreve, Dennis, etc. In doggrel verse. By a Poet. London, 1697, 4to.

Stephen, Leslie. — Congreve. (*Dictionary of National Biography*, vol. xii., pp. 6-9.) London, 1887, 8vo.

Swinburne, Algernon C.—Congreve. (Vol. vi., pp. 271, 272 of the *Encyclopædia Britannica.*) London, 1877, 4to.

——Miscellanies. London, 1886, 8vo.
Congreve, pp. 50-55.

Temple, Richard, *Viscount Cobham.*—Cobham and Congreve. An epistle to Lord Viscount Cobham in memory of his friend Mr. Congreve. London, 1730, 8vo.

Thackeray, William Makepeace.—The English Humorists of the Eighteenth Century, etc. London, 1853, 8vo.
Congreve and Addison, pp. 55-104.

Ward, Adolphus William.—A History of English Dramatic Literature to the death of Queen Anne. 2 vols. London, 1875, 8vo.
William Congreve, vol. ii., pp. 582-589.

Ward, Thomas Humphry.—The English Poets. Selections with critical introductions by various writers, etc. 4 vols. London, 1880, 8vo.
William Congreve. Essay (by Austin Dobson) and Selected Poems, vol. iii., pp. 10-12.

Ware, Sir James. — The whole Works of Sir James Ware. 2 vols. London, 1739-64. Fol.
Congreve, vol. ii., p. 294.

Watkins, John. — Characteristic Anecdotes of Men of Learning and Genius, etc. London, 1808, 8vo.
William Congreve, pp. 420-425.

Wharton, Grace and Philip.—The Wits and Beaux of Society. Second edition. London [1861], 8vo.
William Congreve, pp. 121-143.

Wilson, Charles.—Memoirs of the life, writings, and amours of W. Congreve, Esq., interspersed with miscellaneous essays, letters, etc., written by him. Also some very curious memoirs of Mr. Dryden and his family, with a character of him by Mr. Congreve. London, 1730, 8vo.

Zinck, August G. L.—Congreve, Vanbrugh, og Sheridan. En Skildring til Belysning af de sociale Forhold og det aandelige Liv i England fra Carl den Andens Tid og til henimod den franske Revolution. Kjøbenhavn, 1869, 8vo.

Magazine Articles.

Congreve, William. — Edinburgh Review, by T. B. Macaulay, vol. 72, 1840, pp. 514-528.

——*and Wycherley.*—Gentleman's Magazine, by Charles C. Clarke, vol. 7, N.S., 1871, pp. 823-845.

——*as a Writer of Comedy.* Scots Magazine, vol. 66, 1804, pp. 9-14.

VII. CHRONOLOGICAL LIST OF WORKS.

Incognita; or, Love and Duty reconcil'd . . 1692
Old Bachelor . . . 1693
Double Dealer . . . 1694
Mourning Muse of Alexis . 1695
Love for Love . . . 1695
Pindarique Ode to the King on his taking Namur . 1695
Letter on Comedy . . 1696
Mourning Bride . . 1697
The Birth of the Muse: a poem 1698
Amendments upon Mr. Collier's False and Imperfect Citations . . . 1698
Way of the World . . 1700
The Judgment of Paris: a masque 1701
The Tears of Amaryllis for Amyntas . . . 1705
Pindarique Ode to the Queen 1706
Works (*First Collected Edition*) . . . 1710
Dramatic Works of John Dryden (*Edited*) . . 1717

Letter [in verse] to Viscount Cobham . . 1729